ALSO BY EMILY WHITE

Interning 101

HOW TO BUILD A SUSTAINABLE MUSIC CAREER
AND
COLLECT ALL REVENUE STREAMS

How to Build a Sustainable Music Career and Collect All Revenue Streams

Emily White

9GiantStepsBooks

 @9giantstepsbooks
@9giantsteps

How to Build A Sustainable Music Career and Collect All Revenue Streams

Written by: Emily White

Copyright © 2020 9GiantStepsBooks

This book contains figures and companies that might change in the future. Contact any companies for their current rates as prices evolve. Furthermore, we have provided footnotes for some companies that aren't easily found via an internet search. These footnotes also may change and we will post updates as they arise at the following URL: https://www.9giantstepsbooks.com/SustainableAfterword

FIRST EDITION

For permission requests, write to the publisher, addressed "Attention: Permissions Coordinator," via the website below.

9GiantStepsBooks
Beverly Farms, MA
www.9giantstepsbooks.com

Ordering Information:

Special discounts are available on quantity purchases by corporations, associations, and others. For details, contact the publisher via the website above.

For U.S. trade bookstores and wholesalers order, please contact the publisher via the website above.

Printed in the United States of America

Library of Congress Control Number: 2019921267

How To Build A Sustainable Music Career and Collect All Revenue Streams / Emily White

ISBN Print: 978-0-9993316-2-0
ISBN Digital: 978-0-9993316-3-7

Dedicated to Claudia and Kirk Peterson

CONTENTS

A CONVERSATION BETWEEN ZOË KEATING AND EMILY WHITE

Zoë Keating is the only artist I've ever known who does not need to read this book. She is primarily an instrumental musician who has never made a music video, does not have a manager, and has built a sustainable career for the long term.

In early 2006, I was working at a management company that also had a travel agency for artists and fans. One day, the travel agent came by my desk and told me that Imogen Heap's tour manager had a family emergency and needed to leave the tour immediately. She wanted to know if I could fill in for a few dates. Luckily I had a boss (Mike Luba) who said, "I think that would be a great experience for you!" and off I went to Boston to join Imogen's tour. I've been privileged to tour the globe with artists more times than I can count. Yet this tour was one of the most memorable and life-changing for me. It was three women, including myself, and a sound person on a giant tour bus. Imogen was touring and playing with an incredible musician named Zoë Keating.

I have a vivid memory of Zoë selling out of CD's at the merchandise table early in the tour. She was stressed since so many new fans were discovering her at these shows and frustrated by the great problem of selling more music than usual. I calmly asked where the CD's were stored. They were at her home where Zoë's husband Jeff fulfilled mail orders for her music. I suggested that we essentially set up a merch[1] table "pre-order," letting fans purchase the CD, taking down their name, address, and contact details for Jeff. I've had the pleasure of knowing her career and family intimately ever since.

Zoë Keating is the definition of a modern artist. She has built a sustainable career, which will be discussed in this foreword, and she has all of her revenue streams flowing directly to her. Although Zoë knows that she has built a genuine and deep connection with her audience that defines a sustainable music career, we cannot control the changes that occur around us - both in life and career. Zoë is now a single mother, losing her husband to cancer in 2015. Zoë is a testament to both strength and humanity. She has been publicly navigating new waters with the loss of her partner and shedding light on what it means to be a single parent with a full time music career.

I've looked up to Zoë since I've known her, and I feel it's important to share her career and music with you. She may be new to you, although she has upwards of one million Twitter followers. At the time of this interview, Zoë is writing two film scores during the day and tending to her son after school and at night, all before taking off for London this week. As time is a precious commodity, Zoë and I had a conversation in lieu of a traditional foreword. After her son went to bed, I interviewed her on the tenets of this book and how she does everything I have to say on this subject - on her own.

Zoë and I are both involved in the modern music industry, and we are often placed on the same panels at industry conferences. We tried new music platforms as they became available and figured out how to build

---

1 "Merch" is a term often used in music that is short for "merchandise."

sustainable music careers as we went along. Zoë can also code, and feels that it's the developer in her that led to figuring out her music career. Says Zoë, "I have that programmer's mentally of 'here's a bug, how do I fix it? What's behind this?' Or I look at the system; it's just in my nature. I approach it like I was designing a map or debugging a piece of code." I don't know how to code, but I am an entrepreneur, so I'm all about things that make sense. In music, to me, that means always putting the artist first while taking care of the fans as a very close second. Adds Zoë, "I think there is one thread in all of this for me - whatever is happening in your life and career right now will probably not be happening tomorrow. So it's really good to stay nimble and not be too dogmatic. Things will shift over time." As Zoë has also learned and stated, "No one is going to go out of their way to send you a royalty check."

Zoë has spent the last few years recalibrating around how to now be a single parent and a full time working musician. As such, she is expected to compose and record a score for a television show overnight and through weekends to hit a deadline, while also caring for her son. As Zoë says, "There are 80 or so working composers in Hollywood and a very small percentage are women. There's a reason for that." Or hearing that a film producer wanted to offer her a composing position yet said, "But she's widowed now; she probably won't do it." Even before losing Jeff, there was a shift while becoming a mother as a full time musician when Zoë was asked by a legendary artist to perform at a major annual event a week before her son was due. Six months later, Zoë reached out to the same artist letting him know that she could do it this year and was told, "I didn't think you were doing that any more now that you're a mom;" and that they already had a "female cellist."

Yet Zoë is able to persist professionally and continue to thrive in her career because, as she says, "I have my audience." How did she do that? In this foreword I will take Zoë through the chapters you're about to read to reveal how she did it.

GET YOUR ART TOGETHER

Emily: *How do you know when you're "ripe" and ready to record?*

Zoë: You have to have something to say and you have to be able to execute it. What I notice with artists who are starting out is that often there's a huge gap in what they want to achieve, what they want to do in the studio, and what they can do right now. I had my little time. A bit like when The Beatles went to Germany and were learning their craft. I had my time in the warehouse where I could perform every weekend to an adoring living room audience. And I could make mistakes and learn how to talk to the audience. I wasn't ready to perform. But at some point there was a time when I was ready to go out there and do it. You don't want to go out there until you're ready. That said, I do know some people that hash it out as they go along. But there's also that thing when a band wants to record an album and they're not ready. It's just going to be a waste of money and time.

I can't speak for other artists, but for me, I had a long time of working in private on something. And then I worked really hard on my EP that I was doing. I did it by myself, in a room, and worked on it for quite some time until it was ready. I knew I had made something different that I felt proud of and felt like it represented me as a person. That is when I knew it was something. It wasn't something that I thought was cool or that I liked the sound of. It really felt like this is a musical version of myself. That's when I knew that I was ready to get out there.

However, what happened next had to do with my enthusiasm. I started sending my music out to people I knew in the industry and then I started getting rejections. That's a really difficult point because you have your soul encapsulated in musical form and people are telling you it's not interesting or it doesn't have any marketability. Or maybe you should add vocals to that. Or 'why don't you come into my office and I'll get a picture of you lying across the fur rug and put that on the cover,' which actually happened to me. That's really crushing. So what do you do next?

More likely than not, you're going to be crushed. You're going to think that somebody should hear this musical soul and they're not going to hear what you hear. Because if it's good - maybe it hasn't been done before. And people in the business only want to hear things that they know someone else has done, right? Nearly all the artists I love started doing something that nobody in the industry had heard before and therefore, they weren't ready to hear it yet. So what do you do next? Do you go back to your room and are you going to be crushed? Or are you going to do it yourself? For me, I did it myself. Now that doesn't have to be a linear path. You can do it yourself for awhile and maybe then get a record deal, if that's what you want, or get a publishing deal. Or have some parts of it managed by others. But how do you know when you're ready? Get your art together. Once you start getting your art out there, you're going to get nine no's for every one yes.

PRE-RECORDING MARKETING FOUNDATION: EMAIL LIST, TEXT MESSAGE CLUB, AND SOCIAL MEDIA

Zoë: Email is crucial and it's still amazing at this point when people don't use it. It's just got to be all about the email list and it's worth the money. I pay for the email list every month and I'm happy to pay for it. When I say email list, I also mean text. I don't even put an email list out at shows any more. I put a number out from the stage and place posters with the number in the lobby by the merch table. I'm famous for putting out my email list and losing it. For a while, I was using TaskRabbit for my shows' email list sheets to get the information into my email list's database. Lately I've just been using a text platform, which is great. And *way* more people are signing up that way.

With social media, you might build your audience somewhere and then they're not going to hear from you due to algorithms, because you've given all of your assets over to another company. And who knows if they're going to let that keep working for you. I just did a test with Facebook to pay for a post to have everyone see it. It would cost at least a thousand dollars to get to half of my audience there. That's not feasible.

GET YOUR BUSINESS AFFAIRS TOGETHER BEFORE YOU HIT THE STUDIO AND FAIR COMPENSATION

Zoë: It's very important to discuss what the financial deal is between all of you.

Emily: *Zoë then shared with me a story about a bandmate (not much of a mate in my opinion!) receiving a significant recording advance and not telling Zoë.*

Zoë: I learned a lot of things by making mistakes. It doesn't have to be fraught. People have difficulty talking about money. It's a cultural problem. The only way to do it is just to get through the discomfort and bring it up. Someone has to bring it up. It's going to be awkward until somebody makes the first move. It's always going to be better for you if that's you. It's really, really valuable to know the legal ins and outs in advance of arranging versus writing versus re-mixing, and what those are considered in the world of songwriting splits. It's very important to educate yourself about it, so when you're working you can be thinking, 'Oh, I'm writing; I'm not just arranging.' I certainly didn't know that when I started out, and I think a lot of people still don't. I had a few situations in the film scoring business where I was hired by different well-known composers to do what one of them called "celloifcation." I'd come down with my looping rig and I'd improvise a scene. They would record it and it would make it into the movie. That was composing. But I was only being paid as a session player. Once I realized that, I started saying that I need to be credited. I didn't know the difference at the time; I thought I was just being a session cellist. But actually I was going in there and writing material. And you're right, you can't go and do it afterwards. You can't go later and say to the producer, 'You know that movie I did a session for a year ago? I actually wrote that thing. Can you go back and add my name to the credits? And while we're at it, can I get backend royalty too?' I do have something related I ask for now. Whenever I do something major, I.have 'featuring Zoë Keating' in the song title. The former information architect in me finds that very alarming datawise, because you're mixing different kinds of data in the title. But unfortunately, the way that music metadata works, that is the only way that you can often be searched.

MUSIC PUBLISHING ISN'T SCARY OR CONFUSING + HOW TO LAND A SYNCH[2] PLACEMENT

Zoë: It really is valuable for you as a musician to think about the kind of music you make. Go look at other musicians that are similar to you and see what PRO (Performing Rights Organization) they're signed up with. Because each one has different specialties. Like the TV people are with ASCAP[3] (laughs). Because it's still opaque. They can find you more money, and you want to be with the group who is going to find you more money.

I would say that a lot of the synch placements I've landed have been from playing the cello at all of those tech conferences. So I played at Oracle World for 10,000 people. Somebody saw me there who was putting it on and said 'that music was great,' and they worked for an ad agency. And when they were doing an ad, they said, 'What about that cellist?' So it's been word of mouth. I've never submitted my music to an agency. All of my synchs, which I still continue to get, come from what I call 'manna from heaven,' because it comes out of the sky that way. I think there was a period of time when I was omnipresent in a tech circle and that's when I had my peak licensing. So I did a Chrysler Jeep ad that was for a commercial series called 'Halftime in America' during the Super Bowl and it was directed by Clint Eastwood I believe? And then I did a series of ads for IBM and for Intel. Intel sponsored me for a year; that was great. There were so many other ones like that. Then there are countless films and

2 Short for "synchronization"—a song placed in film, television, a web show, or commercial/advert.

3 American Society of Composers, Authors and Publishers

documentaries. They've been slow and steady. Sometimes more, sometimes less. And I started doing actual scoring in 2008, which is when I did my first full picture. I got a TV show in 2014, which came about in a really funny way. The editors had used my music heavily for the temporary score in the show. They approached a guy, who is now my scoring agent, and said, 'We love the music. Do you have anyone on your roster who is like this?' He said, 'Why don't you just hire her?' And then he went and tracked me down. That's why I'm pretty loyal to him (laughs), because he did that. So that was my first gig and all of the other things I've done thus far is where somebody has used my music and then wanted me to write more for the project. So then I'm working as a composer and also placing a synch.

SETTING UP YOUR RELEASE AND DISTRIBUTION PLAN

Emily: *What does this mean to you?*

Zoë: I think that will change with every release because the technology is changing again. When I released a little EP last year, I was really at a loss. Like, 'Gosh, how do you release music now?' I still feel like we're kind of between formats. Is it really all streaming now? Or should I release the music embedded in a lampshade? Should I sell t-shirts with music in them? It felt like an anachronism, but I ended up doing an informal survey on social media and my email list saying, 'Hey, I have a new thing; what format do you want it in?' I just asked them. Surprisingly people wanted CD's, which I was absolutely not going to make. But that is the one that had the highest percentage of votes. And I sell them; which blows my mind. And I release it on all of the platforms I care about. [Editor's note: Zoë's full catalog is available via Bandcamp and Apple Music.]

But what to do. Am I going to do a pre-order? And then am I going to release it everywhere? There's some nuance in there. You don't have to put it on every platform all at once. There's a lot of pressure from the industry that you have to release everything all at once on every single platform.

Maybe a major artist has to do that if they want to chart, but that's not what we're doing here. If you're a smaller artist, it matters where you release your music first because you might need the money.

Emily then pointed out that one of her company's artists, Julia Nunes, recently made the *Billboard* charts with her own label and owning all of her rights. Zoë then recalled Nielsen contacting her to verify Zoë's information, asking what record label she was on. She explained it was her own imprint, 020202 Music. Zoë asked what this was for and they said, "You're #5 on the *Billboard* classical charts."

HOW TO MARKET WITH OR WITHOUT A BUDGET

Emily: *Do you think about marketing?*

Zoë: No, I don't. I really don't. Maybe that's a problem, but I don't. I'm not saying that's the way forward for everyone.

Emily: *When you put out a release, what do you do after it's out?*

Zoë: I guess I am marketing in a way. My time is marketing, right? I talk about it. And I still feel like my concerts are the best marketing there is. Getting out and performing is the best advertising for me. I still don't sell CD's at shows. I put them out there with a donation box, because what really works for me is when people take a CD and give it to a friend. I make more money with the donation box than I would have if I sold the CD's. And it makes people feel good. Let's see, what else do I do? I've been tweeting.

I'm also the only artist that hasn't made a video, so I don't use YouTube. I think that's just quirky to me. I know that I don't watch videos myself. And if someone sends me their music in video form I'll never listen to it as I can't handle video. I think I'm a highly sensitive person and video is difficult for me. So making a video never occured to me. For a while people would ask me for one. And then I just didn't need it. I'm not opposed to the idea. But it's one of those things where I just haven't used it. In a way I kind of like it because I've entered people's musical consciousness purely with music, which is what I wanted to do from day one. I just wanted to be a musician; I didn't want to make t-shirts. I didn't want to sell any merchandise at all; I just wanted to be all about the music.

There's another thing I'm not talking about, which is being physically shy as a younger person. There was a point in my twenties where I was trying to downplay my femininity on stage because I didn't like the kind of attention I was getting. It made me feel really uncomfortable and I had a few awkward situations. I think I wanted to do everything possible to not be a female in the spotlight. I wanted to de-sexualize myself, or de-sexualize the music. And there's no way to do that in music, unless you do not have music videos done. It wasn't really conscious, but I realize that it's definitely an undercurrent for my music. Then I did have an experience in those early days when I sent my music out. There was a producer who was kind of well known, and I was really excited that he listened to my music. He brought me into his office and he stood there at his desk with his crotch right at my face; it was classic. He had this whole vision on how he was going to package his work just like these other artists he'd produced, who were women. They were all in various states of undress on the cover and all kind of sexy, and I didn't want sex to sell my music. And I felt like I had to do that; like I had to choose. Like women have to choose - what woman are you going to be? Are you going to be the sexy woman? Are you going to be the quirky woman? I decided I'm going to be none of them; I'm just going to be my own weird self. In a way, I feel like me not having a video has become a thing, which is me having control over my own image or lack thereof.

Emily: *That is beautiful, but also ironic. As you consistently receive synch and film / TV / content scoring requests, your music clearly works incredibly well with picture.*

Zoë: Synch and scoring is more than half of my income. Who knows? Maybe because I don't have any videos people are able to think of it. It's almost a joke how many emails I get where people say, 'Your music is *so* perfect for my project.' And the projects are completely different from one another. Yet it speaks to them in some way that they just have to license it. So maybe I feel in some way that the music is my soul in musical form. But it's also a blank slate to put their own image on.

Talking about sustainability - I'm in this for the long game. I want my career to last my entire life. Whatever is happening right now, this second, I just don't care about it. Unless it interests me artistically. I might make a video if for some reason I'm artistically motivated to do it. And then I'm going to make a video the way I make my music, and it would be another representation of what I do. But otherwise I probably won't bother.

YOUR LIVE STRATEGY AND EFFICIENT TOURING
Emily: What has your experience been like touring as a professional musician and a single parent?

Zoë: The school won't let me take my son out of school. Then what do I do? I can't leave him here with a paid caregiver. Which is why I'm at a transition point and figuring out what I'm going to do. In the early days, you bring them with you. On the Imogen Heap tour, I hired sitters in each city, which was $200/night. So if I was doing my own shows it's feasible. But if I'm coming as a session player it isn't. When you're young, get out there and do it. Because as you get on with adult life, it can be difficult to tour.

MERCH RE-CON
Emily: *What is your relationship with merch like?*

Zoë: I'm a hardcore environmentalist and always have been. Early on in my career, in the 90's, I decided I didn't want to sell merchandise because

I didn't want people to buy more stuff. I was delighted when MP3's came along, because I could just make music and didn't have to make a thing. That's the place, [merchandise], where I leave a lot of money on the table. But kind of on purpose, I guess. I don't make much merchandise. I did sell a t-shirt once, because so many people asked. I designed it myself, and did the artwork. I printed them on 100% organic material and found the most expensive, sustainable t-shirt you could find at the time, made in America. It was the most expensive t-shirt on earth (laughs). And lugging those things around was expensive as well, so I decided I wasn't going to do that anymore. I did make a poster, but I had issues with the toxic ink. My newest CD is 100% post-consumer material, even the CD itself. As far as I know, it's impossible to make CD's without the plastic shrinkwrap. Perhaps there is, but I haven't found an option yet for replacing it.

REVENUE STREAM CHECKLIST

Zoë: One thing that I've been meaning to do is tally up all of the income from my most recent recording and see how it has done compared to everything. And it's on my agenda to do this; it has just taken a while. I've been curious - Is it direct to fan via Bandcamp? Is it iTunes? What is the most volume? What is the most money? I know what it is across the board, but I want to know that for my most recent release.

Emily: *Which is exactly why I've created a revenue stream spreadsheet in this book! I want artists to be able to project their monthly and annual incomes realistically, so it can feel like a job - in a good way.*

REPEAT & GROW!

Zoë: You can't expect just because you sold something to someone before, that you can sell something to them again. It's not a given. We all know that with the attention span we have now, people need to have a reason to connect with you. You have to give them a reason. Hopefully you have a relationship with your fans where they *need* to connect with you. That is definitely a plant that needs to be nurtured.

WHEN DO I NEED AN ATTORNEY, BUSINESS MANAGER, AND/ OR A MANAGER? DEFINING AN ARTIST'S TRADITIONAL "TEAM."

Emily: *I think you understand why this chapter is last, with regard to building one's career sustainably and going from there. Do you have these roles in place, and if so or if not, why?*

Zoë: I would say that for an artist, when you start putting things off and that becomes a chronic problem, that means you need help. It's really useful to think about what you're not good at and what you don't like doing and pass those things off to someone else. I don't like negotiating money; I really don't. I can justify my scoring and synch agent's cost because he guaranteed me that he would get me double from what I was getting before. And if he doesn't, we can renegotiate. And it's true, he does. And he loves doing it! My booking agent is the same way. I can't tell you how happy I am. I think it's probably hard to get a recording contact, but it's even harder to get a live booking agent. I feel like live booking agents are actually more valuable. When I got my booking agent, it was such a relief because I was spending so much time researching venues, contacting them, trying to find a way in, creating a fake manager for myself to contact them - the mysterious Mark who doesn't exist. Mark was really good at negotiating money sometimes (laughs). I loved it when I would get licensing gigs. Someone would say, 'We'd like to license your music, how about this much money?' I would just say yes. I didn't know what else to do. It was really hard for me to switch into business mode. So those are two people that I have, an agent for synch and film scoring, and an agent for live performance bookings. I also would not do my own legal services and am very happy to pay my attorney. When I used to find out about, say a major ballet company using my music without licensing, I used to get really depressed. Now I feel good about it. Oh and I don't do my own accounting. Though all of the money comes in here, and I organize and code expenses, my accountant handles my taxes for me. I used to do all of those things, all of the pieces. But in general, as soon as you start pushing things off because you can't deal, make an honest list of what you don't like doing and what you're not good at. And see if you can give that to someone else [who is reputable] to work on.

Emily: *But you essentially are your own manager. You're the C.E.O. of all of it.*

Zoë: I think so. I don't always like being my own manager. But I think that I know what motivates me more than anyone. Only I can look at something and know if it makes my heart sing and that I want to get involved. Or only I can look at something and know that I'm not going to be able to do it. That's not to say that I make all of the decisions by myself. I do ask people for advice. I have a group of friends, and when something comes up, we talk through an opportunity and I see what they think about it. I use to be really down on myself for not being able to do long term strategic planning. And I've let that go in a major way. I've come to believe and understand that you can have structures in your life to help keep things going. But things are going to fall apart. And there's often not anything you can do about it. And you're just going to be beating yourself up about it. I think there's this illusion of control that we have and I realize that part of going through what I've been through is that we don't have a lot of control. What you can control is how you feel about something. So for strategic planning for my career, I can have in my mind that I want to do something next year, but then it might come up that the school superintendent might not let me take my son on tour. So what do I do with that? I've stopped doing that to some degree. I'm not planning tours and work so far in advance. I have another person in the world that I have to care for. And it's not always good for him to plan something that's a year away. I'm back to being a little more ad hoc than I used to be.

■ ■ ■

Thank you Zoë, from the bottom of my heart. For your time, and for all that you do for your family, all of us, and countless people around the world.

So much love,
Emily xoxo

INTRODUCTION

The music industry was set up decades ago to confuse artists. What's exciting about the modern music industry—and by modern, I mean the time since music evolved from physical to digital—is that artists can now not only create and distribute music on their own, but they in theory have transparent access to all of their revenue streams.

However, I rarely meet artists who have all of their revenue streams organized in one place that they can access so they know how much money is coming in, as well as what they can anticipate financially based on those revenue streams moving forward. And I get it. I'm an entrepreneur too. I know what it's like to get a chunk of money and be happy with that because it means I can go back to doing what I love, which is creating things I want to see in the world. But that's not any way to run or build a long-term and sustainable career as an entrepreneur and/or an artist.

I have a deep understanding of how to build a sustainable career in the modern music industry. And, to be clear, this information is out there. I've had the absolute privilege of speaking at countless music business conferences around the globe. I see artists at SXSW, Midem, and beyond in the audience furiously taking notes, grasping at nuggets of information (e.g., "This is what publishing is. This is what SoundExchange is.") Yet I've never seen a conference put all of the information that artists need to build a sustainable career and collect on all of their revenue streams *in order* from say, steps one to ten. I've expressed this concern to conferences, and the common responses are understandable. Such as, "We only had access to so many rooms, so we had to set up competing panels." Or, "X person couldn't arrive until the last day of the conference, so they had to speak then."

What this results in is educating artists on their own careers in a convoluted order. Explaining how to build a career and collect on all revenue streams based on a business that was initially set up to confuse artists is a feat similar to teaching children multiplication and division before they learn addition and subtraction. Having this information presented in a completely arbitrary order is super confusing for any artist trying to walk away fully versant in the music business.

Similarly, almost every artist I meet wants me to explain all of this to them. I've hesitated on writing this book for a long time, only out of concern that the information can get outdated quickly. However, my last straw was when a successful retired Olympic swimmer asked me if I wouldn't mind talking to his college-aged musician daughter about her career. I didn't mind. But you shouldn't have to be an Olympian's daughter, or know me personally, to have access to this information.

Thus, my second book was born.

In this book, I will explain how to build a sustainable career in the modern music industry and ensure you're not missing a single revenue stream. We'll go from start to finish (then repeat!), from A to Z, one to ten, however you want to describe a methodical order. This book isn't designed for you to "choose your own adventure" or skip around. Read it in order, follow the instructions, and you will learn the most robust ways to build a long-term and sustainable music career.

Let me add that the music industry is not evil. When I opened this introduction by saying, "The music industry was set up decades ago to confuse artists," I'm talking about the pre-digital business structures that were created to make anyone's head spin. The actual industry *had* to exist in the physical era, as record companies essentially controlled access to recording because studios were far too expensive for anyone who wasn't a 1-percenter to hire. Similarly, labels controlled access to the distribution of music when it was a physical object.

The digital era has cracked this all wide open, both for artists and for those who work in the music industry. I feel that many of the industry people who remain in the digital era are the ones who are truly in the music business for the right reasons. That doesn't mean we haven't lost some great humans to other fields along the way! But those in the music industry who are currently in it for the long haul, for the most part, can't imagine doing anything else and truly want to help artists succeed. At the same time, there isn't a single manager, agent, label, or any industry person who is a miracle worker. Generally speaking, we're here to help you. But if scoring one or all of these roles meant instant success, then the countless artists who have attained teams would all be successful. That obviously isn't the case. I'm explaining my thoughts on modern industry professionals so you understand that this book isn't pro- or anti- music industry, as falling into cut-and-dry camps like that isn't the point.

I'm here to teach you how to build a long-term career whether you have music industry professionals involved or not. And if you do have a team or obtain team members along the way, you should *still* follow the fundamental guidelines I lay out, as these team members may come and go for a variety of reasons. Yet no matter who is on your team, isn't the goal to have a long-term career and collect all of the revenue you are owed forever? That's exactly the point of this book. I've taken the disparate bits of information that are out there and put them together to explain building a sustainable career as a musician in an orderly and straightforward manner.

I've been at the forefront of the evolution of the modern/digital music industry as an artist manager and entrepreneur. Yet the revolution that many saw happening has left a bit of a mess, despite a manifold of great intentions. So, yes, educate yourself, read my colleagues' books, go to conferences if you want a deeper dive. But all of that is incredibly overwhelming, time consuming, and the costs add up. The only reason I know how to do all of this is because I've dug in and tried just about every tool and new platform available for the artists I've worked with throughout my career. I've navigated these waters and have laid out the information that I deeply believe is best for artists' careers in order.

Hence, if you want to learn how to build a career from day one, this book is for you. If it isn't the dawn of your career, I'll teach you how to get things organized, while also ensuring that all of your past revenue streams are being collected on and paid to you moving forward.

Here we go!

CHAPTER 1:

GET YOUR ART TOGETHER

First and foremost, one must make great art to be successful. Something inside compelled you to pick up this book, which means you have a creative spirit within. What's exciting to me about the modern music industry is that anyone can have a career, and now, more than ever before, careers come in a variety of sizes. This is because musicians can now record and distribute on their own, and therefore, the amount of people doing so is basically infinite. In the pre-digital era, I used to know every popular artist and song no matter the genre because what was available to listen to was essentially finite. Today, it would be impossible to know all of the artists making music just within the genres I tend to primarily work in.

With more music and content in the world than ever, one must truly be great to build a career at any level. At the same time, anyone who does so can have a career. There are no limits on what to create, as the vast majority of musicians making art today aren't legally bound to any sort of "approval" of their music before release. Think of all of the subgenres that exist in EDM (electronic dance music) alone. Whether it's a solo songwriter or someone making beats at home, the sky is truly the limit on the type of art that you can put into the world.

Therefore, before you even move on to the next chapter—get your art together. "Pitch sessions," where artists can play their music to industry types like me, happen frequently at conferences. More often than not, the artist says, "I really need to work on my vocals, get a new drummer," or some other additional issue that they know they need to resolve before the music is ready to share. In this instance, I understand that they're excited to play the music for an "industry" person, but regardless, this happens all too often. It's cliché, but don't put the cart before the horse. Your music is the horse, and the cart isn't going anywhere without it.

You know better than anyone when the art that you're making is the full and true expression of yourself and ready for the world.

That said, I also hear from artists who want my "feedback" on their music. There are people in the industry who have incredible ears for their areas of expertise. A dear friend who is a radio promotions genius comes to mind. One of his many clients is a legendary label head who does not make a decision on who to sign without consulting my friend. So much so that when the aforementioned label head passed on The Lumineers, my friend jumped up and down and pounded on the label head's desk, saying, "This is a hit! This is a hit!" My radio promotions guru friend was right, and this is because he has a unique talent and years of experience knowing what appeals to radio stations' program directors.

Lauren Ross is another person with such a talent. Lauren has been landing synch placements since college for the record label Kill Rock Stars and went on to the same great work at Terrorbird Media for artists of her choosing. A "synch" or "synchronization placement" is music used in a film, on television, a web show, or advertisement. I sent Lauren an artist once and didn't hear back. No big deal, as she's as busy as anyone in the industry. A few months later, she wrote me back, sending her deepest apologies for the delay as she'd finally had a chance to listen. She was extremely excited and confident, as she knew she could land the band a variety of synch placements. Lauren went on to do just that and it is still, to this day, the artist's number one revenue stream.

I highlight these talented industry colleagues, as those with a keen ear are absolutely out there. But for me as a manager, I love what I love and know that we can build a sustainable career for any artist who truly makes great art (and has a great attitude and wants to connect with their fans, but more on that later). This may sound counterintuitive, but never in my career have I set out for an artist to have a "hit" song. When it happens, it's awesome. And when it happens, my mind immediately goes into data-collection mode, running around ensuring we are capturing as much contact information as possible for fans and tastemakers who are now exposed to the artist. This is in hopes that we can entice said fans and tastemakers to support the artist for the long haul, especially if the next track isn't a hit. One could argue that this thinking doesn't make sense if your goal is to be a pop star. However, an artist like Robyn comes to mind. Robyn is huge, don't get me wrong, but I also know that she is beloved and respected by many in the indie music and critical darling scene. As of this writing, she has a Twitter following in the 370,000 range. In chapter 7, we will talk about how large social media numbers do not necessarily mean success, but regardless, 370,000 is relatively low for a global pop star. What I mean by this is, Robyn is a pop star that has absolutely had hits. But she has built a career that is consistently strong over time, which I feel is a goal all artists should strive for. As mentioned, hit songs are great. They also come and go. The point of this book is to give you the tools and knowledge so your career lasts for as long as you want it to.

And if you want to be a pop star? Lady Gaga and Taylor Swift are incredible at connecting with their audiences. Taylor has hosted listening parties for her most hardcore fans and hangs out on Tumblr to comment and engage with many of her countless fans on a personal level. Therefore, even some of the largest pop stars on the planet are following the strategies laid out in this book. And if these artists' mainstream audiences reject their music at any point, their true fans will be there for them in the long run, as they've cultivated relationships with said fans to ensure this. I also get the impression that both Gaga and Taylor enjoy these interactions with their fans and do not shy away from them.

My point on all of the above is that more often than not, artists with life-long careers are authentically themselves. They're not trying to be something they are not and aren't making music that they think they're supposed to make. Great art comes from within, and being genuine to your vision and spirit is going to be what connects with people. Anything else isn't going to last for the long haul.

So it's time to get your music together before I teach you how to build a career. Get your songs together, (assuming you're a songwriter, and if you're not, get your writers and/or co-writers together), and figure out how you want to make the music you have in mind. Do you want to be a band or group? A solo artist who hires a band? There are pros and cons to both.

Being in a band is really hard. You have a group of human beings, and life is going to intercede at one point or another—whether it's that someone wants to pursue more education, starts a family and needs to be at home to do so, or frankly life just flat out happening. It is rare, if ever, that multiple people can become a unit for years on end without normal life elements arising that might take priority. Which is fine! Know that these issues arise in all bands. If you do want to be in some sort of group, I'll explain in chapter 3 how to ensure that everyone is getting their fair share. But for now, we're talking about figuring out how to get your art together. And if a band or group is the best way to do so, then go for it!

Don't get me wrong. Being a solo artist is also challenging. Plenty of renowned artists that you have heard of struggle with the costs of touring, as they need to hire musicians for the road. Regardless, the point of this chapter is to encourage you to get your art together. Only you know what that truly means. If you are in a group or a band, it means that you have all creative elements in place and are ready to start building your career. And if you're solo, it means getting together the songs, music, and players that will put your best foot forward for the vision you have in mind.

Once your art is in a place where you're ready to say to my radio promo friend, Lauren, or myself, "This is the music I am so proud of, and is the best representation of who I am, what I do, and what I want to create and put into the world," then you're ready. To be clear, any industry person or musician can hear something great, powerful, and impactful, almost no matter the recording quality. I say "almost," as we don't want the music file to be so low resolution that even a non-audiophile like me is distracted from your work because it's so compressed. But any great artist or songwriter will come through with basic recording tools that we'll lay out in chapter 4, and you certainly don't need to book Abbey Road Studios to do so.

There isn't a single artist or creative soul who doesn't know what I mean by all of the above. So get your art together. When you know that you've come up with the greatest possible music that you are ready to put into the world, then you're ready to go.

CHAPTER 2:

PRE-RECORDING MARKETING FOUNDATION: EMAIL LIST, TEXT MESSAGE CLUB, AND SOCIAL MEDIA

Congrats! If you've made it here, that means your music is ready to go. Before you dive into recording, which I know you're excited to do, let's get organized so the foundation is in place for your release to be as successful as possible.

The Power of Email

First up—do you have an email list? If not, create one immediately. Ask friends, family, and fans if it's OK to add their email addresses to your list. Let them know that this is the most direct way to keep them informed on your music. I've often said that an artist's email list is their retirement plan. We're going to talk about social media in this chapter, as it's a great way to market and communicate, but you do not own your social media accounts—technology companies do. To put this in perspective, what if you'd built your fanbase on Friendster? (If you're old enough to remember the first mainstream social networking site.) More relevant, what if your MySpace page was the sole place you built your fanbase? I know it's hard to believe, but these examples prove that the social media we rely on today might not exist in the future. I've been saying this for years and although it used to feel unthinkable, it's more than possible that Facebook will not exist in the future or in the form it does now. The average Facebook user's age continues to rise. (Not that we don't love fans of all ages!) And as the platform continues to be embroiled in privacy scandals and users start to understand the power of their own data, Facebook and all social media companies will undoubtedly change and evolve over time.

What you *do* own and control is your email list. So start *now*. In college, I worked with a band called The Dresden Dolls. This was *way* before email lists were heavily discussed at marketing conferences in every field. Amanda Palmer of the band began by gathering emails to keep people informed of their shows when the band started, which were often at art galleries, parties, and not at traditional venues. Amanda had the foresight to understand this direct connection to her audience, again well before anyone was talking about such a thing, and would say to me, "What if you go away? What if my fancy booking agent goes away? What if my attorney goes away?" And so on. "This is the *only way* I have to communicate with the fans about our music and shows."

Not only was Amanda right, but both her and Brian Viglione of the band had, and still have, that mind-set. You could barely say hi to either of them, or me, at the merchandise table in those days without one of us saying, "Would you like to sign up for our email list?" It's an engaging thing for a merchandise person to say to fans when they're hovering around the merch table as well. You can also offer fans a sticker, button/badge, or other fun item as a reward for signing up. We'll talk more about this for your touring strategy later in the book, but your email list should be sturdy and part of your gear list for all shows. And don't forget to import the email addresses after you collect them all!

If connecting with fans isn't enticing enough for you to build an email list, know that I feel it's an artist's retirement plan for a reason. When Amanda was prepping the release of her debut solo album, I grabbed, (with permission), The Dresden Dolls' email list. All of those asks at the merch table added up, as by 2008, the band had over fifty thousand email addresses and has thousands more today. Amanda, who was signed to a major label subsidiary, sold ten-thousand copies of her record in the first week. Roughly one thousand were sold by the record company, with over nine thousand fans buying the new album directly from Amanda's website and email list. Absolutely no offense to the people at the record company, but in theory, their job was to sell records. Yet it was Amanda and the band's strong email list that sold 90 percent of the albums in the first week. Not to mention that we built in creative bundles for the audience. Due to this, the artist ended up grossing six figures in a week thereby keeping the vast majority of that income. As luckily, the label did not have rights to any of her merchandise used to create the bundles.

I promise we'll be making music soon. But before you begin, get your email list in place, and have the mind-set that signing everyone you come into contact with up for it is more important financially for you in the long term than, say, people streaming your music.

There are many email list platforms out there, and I generally advise artists to use one of two, based on their situation. MailChimp is free to get started, so most start there. If you or someone you know is decent at graphic design, they will love MailChimp. I've had interns and team members initially struggle with using MailChimp, so if you are not technical (a.k.a. do not know how to code), be patient as you get set up. However, like any technology, MailChimp gets more user-friendly every day, so I encourage you to check it out.

FanBridge is the other company that we use often, as it was built from day one with musicians in mind. There is a fee to use FanBridge, so you may want to start with MailChimp. But know that FanBridge is cheaper once you have over two-thousand subscribers. Therefore, we often see artists start with MailChimp and move over to FanBridge once their list grows over two thousand. I've also had non-technical team members find FanBridge's templates to be more user-friendly than MailChimp's. However, if you know how to code, most technical folks prefer MailChimp's UX (user experience).

Text Message Collection

Truth be told, I tried over a decade ago to build a text-based fan list for an artist, before such a platform officially existed. Now there are companies such as Textedly, SuperPhone, EZTexting, Fangage, Digits, Twilio.com, and Reach that support you in building up such a list. Data is showing that voter turnout increases with text communication versus email lists, and I recommend communicating this way to your fans as well. Keep this in mind, as technology evolves, as well as for what is best for your fanbase. Don't get me wrong, ideally you need to have an email list and text club, to appeal to all fans. At the same time, just about everyone has a mobile phone on them, and texting is often less cumbersome than email.

Your Social Media Foundation

Next up, let's get your social media platforms in place. We'll talk much more about social media strategy in chapter 7, but for now, ensure that you have an artist Facebook page, Twitter account, and Instagram. If you feel drawn to Snapchat and/or TikTok, great. If they're not for you, don't sweat skipping them. I'd also recommend grabbing a YouTube page at this time. Ideally, you should ensure that all of your social media handles, (e.g. I'm @EmWizzle), are the same across platforms and set up custom URL's that also match that handle. If the handle is taken, get creative, but try to be as consistent as possible so your fans can easily find you. I rarely meet an artist at this point who doesn't have their social media accounts in place, but if this is new and you don't know where to begin, please check out Ariel Hyatt's books. They are a wonderful road map to learn how to set up your social media from a musician's perspective from day one.

We want you to have your email list, text club, and social media in place from the get go so you can keep your fans engaged throughout the recording process. If you hop right into recording mode and suddenly want to connect, you'll have to waste precious creative time doing all of the above. Get your social media accounts in place now so you can fully immerse yourself in the creative process of recording your music.

Monetizing from Day One

If you have a clear vision for your music release with regard to what it will be—say, a single, an EP, or album—I want you to set up a pre-order before you commence recording and launch it as soon as you hit the studio. I know you got into music to create great art. I want you to keep creating great art, and the point of this book is to teach you how to collect on all of your revenue streams. Therefore, let's start monetizing your music from day one of its existence. Also *please* do not limit yourself to the traditional formats I mentioned (single, EP, album). The sky is truly the limit in the modern era! You can release a song a day, a song a month culminating in a vinyl release after twelve months, or whatever you want. No matter your vision for your music, if you have one for this release, set up a pre-order. If you don't have a clear picture of your music release's format yet, do not fret! We have a monetization plan for you as well.

There are a variety of services that can help you set up your pre-order. But you will retain the most revenue by doing it yourself. If you know how to code, use CASH Music's incredible tools. (Full disclosure, I'm on their board.) If you don't know how to code, like me, I've enjoyed seamlessly selling content directly via websites hosted by Squarespace. Admittedly, like anything, the platform takes a little bit of getting used to. But once you get the hang of it, it's very easy to set up and sell content directly through a Squarespace website, which will also be *your* website where you can post tour dates, news, and whatever you want.

Putting Monetization Where My Mouth Is

We're taking the same advice with this book. To help my publisher offset the costs of artwork and an editor, we launched a pre-order for the book within a week of when I began writing it. It's been fun to keep those who are interested in this project engaged as I go, and I've set out a clear plan to complete and deliver the book. I don't think one needs to stress about an exact release date, but it's important to give the audience a rough idea of when they can anticipate the release. In my case, we have shared the Introduction, so people have an idea of the information that the book will contain, and they therefore know what they are pre-ordering.

Authentic Fan Engagement

In your case, if you want to share an early demo or something that is exciting and special for the fans, great! Though, I also completely understand if you want to keep the music under wraps until it is ready. However, what you can do is keep your pre-order fans engaged with photos, video snippets, and teasers from the studio as you create, so they feel like a part of the process. And if and when life arises for you, the fans know that too. If, god-forbid, you have a tragedy arise throughout this process, you can share that with the audience (without sharing the specifics if you don't want to), so they know why a delay in release might occur.

Sustainable Pre-Orders on Third Party Websites

If setting up a pre-order via Squarespace is something you know you cannot do, (and although I'm an "expert" in this, setting up the pre-order for this book took me about an hour; I promise it's not hard. I encourage you to give it a shot.), I suggest building your pre-order on IndieGoGo.com or Kickstarter. I list IndieGoGo first, as you will keep the funds that you raise no matter what. In Kickstarter's case, your goal must be obtained to receive the funds. The antidote to this is to put your own funds in if you don't reach your Kickstarter goal, but that's often counterintuitive, as the point of these platforms is to raise money that you don't have for your project.

What *is* great about all of the above platforms is that you will retain email addresses for all of your fans, which is not the case if you set up a pre-order with a major technology company such as Apple Music. We're going to talk about Bandcamp as a tool for direct-to-fan in chapter 6, but for now, your largest profit margin will be directly from your website.

How to Build Your Pre-Order Campaign

Where does one begin when building a pre-order campaign? You want to have a price point for everyone, and also ensure that your profit margins don't get cannibalized by expensive manufacturing processes. So get creative! And think about what *you* are into as a fan of other artists or anyone that you admire. At the dawn of the "direct-to-fan" era, around 2010, I remember Arcade Fire releasing an album with a variety of tiers. In theory, I would have been fine with the digital download option. (Reminder that this was the pre-streaming era.) But each tier grew so enticing that suddenly I was spending $100 for a bunch of items surrounding the album that I thought sounded awesome. Keep all of this in mind as you build your pre-order. Make sure lower priced items are included and bundled into higher priced tiers. This ensures that your pre-order makes sense as the audience reads your campaign and gets more excited with every tier's offering.

Here are some suggested pre-order and sales tiers:

- $8: Digital download. This amount undercuts iTunes' traditional album price. Offer to get this out to fans no later than the day of your official release. An added bonus is releasing your digital music and art to these early supporters twenty-four to forty-eight hours ahead of digital service providers, or "DSPs," such as Spotify, Apple, etc.

- $15: CD plus digital download. It feels absurd to write this, as I don't have a CD player. But I manage Julia Nunes, who recently sold one-thousand CDs in an album pre-order, so this demand does exist. Not to mention that I'm hearing of this demand from distribution companies, as well from articles on how CDs are popular in various parts of the world. Therefore, let's not deny fans this option.

- $25: Vinyl. We'll give you manufacturing options for vinyl in chapter 6, so do not worry if you don't know how to do this. And every vinyl company I've ever worked with includes a digital download, but make sure to offer that option in all tiers moving forward so your fans score the digital download as soon as it's available.

- $35 to $50: Autographed vinyl or CD. Start at $35 if it's early in your career, and feel free to increase the price as your profile rises.

- $75: Autographed vinyl or CD plus a thank-you note from you. Who wouldn't want a thank-you note from an artist they are into? This is such a simple and thoughtful gesture that won't break the bank to create.

- $100: Autographed vinyl or CD plus a custom outgoing voicemail message.

- $125: Autographed vinyl or CD plus thank-you note from you and personalized video thank-you message. Again, the video is really special and something that you can create with a smartphone or laptop.

- $150: Autographed vinyl or CD plus name in the liner notes.

- $175: Autographed vinyl or CD plus signed setlist, video shout-out message to a fan filmed at the tour stop of their choice, and name in the liner notes.

- $200: Autographed vinyl or CD plus signed handwritten lyric sheet and name in the liner notes.

- $250: Autographed vinyl or CD plus thank-you-note from you, personalized video dedicated to the fan, and name in the liner notes.

- $500: All of the above plus vinyl test pressing (limited to two).

I'll leave it there based on where you are at in your career. Just this week I saw an artist play video games with his fans as a reward, and another offer a "roadie for a day" experience. The aforementioned Amanda Palmer went on to launch the highest-grossing Kickstarter in history for a musician, grossing over $1 million USD, largely based on higher price points. So if building in private house shows makes sense for you, add that. There is so much you can do here, but these choices are up to you. Remember, it's crucial for your relationship with your fans that you fulfill all items. So be mindful to not overload yourself and communicate with those who ask questions about the pre-order.

Shipping and Fulfillment

Note that Squarespace will let you create shipping options for fans to choose from, so fulfillment costs do not come out of the price points you set. With IndieGoGo or Kickstarter, you will have to build in shipping costs. Postage and packaging costs can vary, especially depending on where you get mailers/boxes/bubble wrap, etc. Rate calculators are not quite foolproof either. For self-fulfilling artists and those getting started on a limited or non-existant budget, I recommend purchasing packaging in bulk from Amazon or a big box retailer to save on these expenses.

And before you launch, don't forget to test your pre-order so you know the experience is good to go for your audience. It might look ready, but you could easily forget to add shipping, international options, or even payment information for yourself so the platform knows where to send your funds. Many direct to fan sites offer free test orders, but you can also use a real card and refund yourself.

Patreon

If your music is ready to go for recording, but you *don't* have a clear vision of what the release will be (e.g., a single, EP, album, etc.), that's OK too! In this scenario, I encourage you to set up a Patreon page immediately. Patreon is based on the concept of being a "patron" of the arts and supporting creators. Set up and launch your Patreon page so your community (even if it's friends and family at first, as we all need to start somewhere) can support you and stay connected with what you're creating as the process evolves.

You can also set up your pre-order through Patreon; though I really like keeping everything on your own website as much as possible, as you own and control it. Patreon has had some (since cleared up) payment issues for creators and also currently charges $0.35 per transaction in addition to a percentage. That said, definitely set up a Patreon page if you aren't quite sure what kind of release you're setting up, so people can still support you as you hit the studio.

If you do have a clear vision for your pre-order and go the artist website route but then your recording process takes longer than expected with a lull in pre-order activity, definitely launch a Patreon so your fans can support you to the finish line of your release. If you're on track with your recording, launch a Patreon shortly after your release date. That way fans can support you and stay involved as you theoretically travel and spread the word on the art you just created.

You could also create a "fan club" on your own where fans support you directly via PayPal. However, if you get paid via Patreon's direct deposit option, the commission is similar to PayPal's, so you might as well use Patreon's platform, as it's already set up and ready to go. Not to mention that many fans know what Patreon is and are happy to sign up and support you.

Pre-order/Patreon Launch

Once your pre-order and/or Patreon plan is together, use your afore-mentioned email list, text club, and social media accounts to share your pre-order link and let fans know that you're commencing creating music! This way you've given yourself a chance to monetize your music from day one, and you can continue to excite and engage with your audience throughout the recording process. Keep in mind utilizing Instagram Live and Facebook Live when making major announcements, so you can do so via live video.

Now it's *almost* time to make some music! In the next chapter, we'll help you to talk about the financial plan with any band members, hired musicians, co-writers, producers, and engineers. This ensures that all of the backend work is discussed *before* you begin recording, instead of after the fact, which can hold up your release. *Then* we'll finally get to the magic of creating music.

CHAPTER 3:

GET YOUR BUSINESS AFFAIRS TOGETHER AND FAIR COMPENSATION

The Business of Recording

Before you commence recording, it is crucial that you sort out how everyone will be compensated. Far too many artists wait until they are in the middle of or done with recording, which often leads to a convoluted mess. I know that money isn't many people's favorite topic to discuss. But I guarantee that you are making your life easier by getting this squared away before you begin recording. It can be a nightmare and also hold up your release if you do so later.

In the following chapter, we're going to talk about how to record with or without a budget. If you do not have a recording budget and feel that you need one, launch your pre-order right away, letting your audience know that they are funding your music. You can also do a straightforward direct-to-fan, Kickstarter-esque campaign and let them know you are raising funds to create the art. But again, we're going to teach you how to record with reasonable costs in the modern era, so this isn't necessarily required.

If you do not have a recording budget and know that you're going to record at home and on your own, but do have band/group members, players, and/or a producer and/or engineer(s) to compensate, what follows are suggestions on how to take care of what is known as business affairs.

Master Recording and Publishing Rights

In a recorded song, there are two "rights" involved. The master recording, and the songwriting, or publishing. I will define publishing in a clear way in chapter 5 and teach you how to collect your revenue on it. But to support the information in this chapter, I'm clarifying up front what both "sides" of rights involved in making music are.

Traditional Master Ownership

For your future reference, the best way to get "signed," if that is a goal (which we'll talk about at the end of the book), is to do everything you can on your own, which is what this book is all about. If you do enter into a label agreement, independent labels are generally a fifty/fifty deal on the master recording after recoupment. Some own the master in perpetuity (forever). Others revert the master as a license back to the artist at some point—if it is recouped and the artist gives notice to the label per the terms of their contract. Generally speaking, a major label deal will give 15 percent of the master recording's revenue to the artist after recoupment and 85 percent to the label. Note that a major label will now more often than not want ownership of more of your rights not limited to publishing, touring, and merchandising. This is a quick primer on master recording ownership so you understand what is out there while we teach you the option of how to own your master, if that's of interest.

Extra "Points" / Percentages for Your Recording Team When You Truly Cannot Afford Their Cash Rates

Generally, unless you are a band/group, the musicians, producers, and engineers you work with are going to appreciate it if you can pay them something. Any sort of cash gesture that you can afford will go a long way. But what you can do, if you truly cannot afford their full cash rate, is reward these folks with points (which means a percentage) on the *master recording*. *Not* on publishing, unless they legitimately co-write a song with you. One incredible element of the modern music industry is that artists can now own and control their master recordings. Again, this was literally all but impossible in the pre-digital era, give or take Fugazi or Ani DiFranco. So if you don't have a ton of cash, see if your players and producer or engineers are open to more points on the master than what they would receive otherwise, if at all.

Assuming you are a solo artist, I'd like for you to keep at least 50 percent of your master recordings' royalty share. That gives you, assuming you own your master recording, another 50 percent to compensate those who worked on the record, if they aren't being paid much or anything up front.

For example, if you are working with four players, a producer, and an engineer, I'd propose allotting 5 percent, or five "points," for the engineer (which is very high for an engineer, but this is if there truly is no cash budget) and splitting the rest equally among the players and producer, so they each receive nine points, or 9 percent on the master recording. That keeps it pretty fair for everyone. I'm also making an assumption here that your producer is up to mix and use mastering software for your recordings. To be clear, I understand that ideally these roles are handled by different people. But I also want to ensure we're discussing options for all budgets, or lack thereof.

If you aren't spending any money on marketing, these points and percentages can come off of the top of revenue from your recordings. This encompasses your direct-to-fan, Bandcamp, and digital service provider revenue (Spotify, Apple Music, Tidal, etc.), SoundExchange royalties, as well as synch placements on the master recording side. Note that these are revenue streams that we will cover how to set up and collect on in later chapters of this book. If you spend funds on promotion for the album, such as a publicist or social media ads to drive people to the music, these percentages should be paid after these costs are recouped (reimbursed) by the recording revenue that has come in. That said, make sure your players, producer, and engineers know about this in advance. As you should take care of these folks first, or let them know "I have x amount of money and was hoping to use it on social media ads and a publicist to promote the music. How can we best compensate you *and* promote the music for everyone's benefit?" In that instance, maybe they do it for half of their cash rate, but also additional points, as mentioned in this section. Or again, if there is truly no budget for anything, suggest points up front in lieu of cash and let them know there are no promotion costs to stand behind - the music will be pure revenue from day one. Though, these payments should come after you recoup any cash fee you pay up front to a distribution aggregation company, which is generally in the $30-49 USD range. And in the producer and mixer's case, who will generally receive a percentage on the master side when they're receiving their full cash rates, make sure they get more points than what they'd receive otherwise per industry standards. I will lay out standard producer and mixing engineer points in this chapter. This is as opposed to players, who wouldn't necessarily have a right to points up front, as hired session musicians are traditionally paid in cash.

If you are in a band or a group, I suggest offering the producer ten points if they aren't receiving any cash or their full cash rate up front, and offering a mixing or studio engineer (if your producer isn't covering these roles), five points if they're not receiving their full cash rate. Again, I feel that solo artists should retain at least 50% of their master recording points to help support promotion costs, splitting the remaining points equally amongst your players when there is truly no cash budget. Similarly, groups and bands can share in the remaining master recording points after you've decided how to compensate your producer and engineers in a no or low cash budget. I recommend splitting the remaining points equally between yourself and group or band members in situations where there isn't a cash budget to compensate them for playing on the recording. All of this is whatever you want it to be. But frankly, what I'm proposing is keeping fairness and equality amongst all involved in mind for those on the recording to avoid infighting.

Points / Percentages for Producers and Mixing Engineers When You Pay Full Cash Rates

If you do you have some sort of a budget to compensate everyone, even better! Start with your producer, as they may have the highest cash rate of anyone on your recording team. For a point of reference, I manage producers who are in some of the biggest bands in the world. These are established "names" with extensive reels and recording resumes, who will work within budgets. But despite their stature, generally speaking, they're comfortable with a rate of $1,000 per track plus their standard producer points, which we'll discuss. I'm throwing this out there because unless your producer is at that level, be mindful of being overcharged. Again, this is negotiable, but it crushes my soul when I see new producers charging an arm and a leg to artists when they don't have the reel/resume/CV to back it up.

Producers are also entitled to producer "points." A local/new producer generally receives 1 to 2 percent *on the master recording.* (Again, we'll talk about publishing shortly.) Someone with a few titles under their belt should receive 3 percent. A producer who has worked with national acts should receive 4 percent. And your Mark Ronsons/St. Vincents/Dr. Dres/Rick Rubins of the world are entitled to 5 percent. Please reread that last sentence. If you are not working with a producer that everyone in music has heard of, and the producer is receiving their full cash rate up front, I do not feel they should be receiving more than five points.

Many producers and their attorneys will push back if you are not "signed," and will ask for more than the percentages for producers that I've laid out, even when you're paying their full cash rate. As your career grows, you will gain the leverage to push back on this. Artists whom I've mentioned so far in this book such as Zoë Keating, The Dresden Dolls, Julia Nunes (as well as countless others not named in this book) have the leverage to do just that. This is because their releases can easily generate as much, if not more, income than those signed to a traditional label. And the remaining 50% of the master recording percentage share I encourage you to hang onto can help to fund promotion - which is exactly what a label's job is.

I'm fascinated by those who ask for more points because an artist is unsigned. There are so many examples of artists signed to labels and it not working out, that I feel this position is antiquated and just plain isn't reality in the modern era. For example, if an artist raises a significant amount of funds on Kickstarter or via a direct-to-fan pre-order to pay for promotion that a traditional label would otherwise handle, why should a producer then receive exponentially more points than they would with a label? Working with a label or any partner does not guarantee success. Thus, as your fanbase grows and you gain knowledge and leverage over your career on how to promote and monetize your music, you can now point this out to anyone who isn't a "name" that is asking for far more points than what I've laid out above. If you're just getting started, you won't yet have this leverage. But point out that you are essentially funding your release's label and promotion. And the more points that go to the producer, the less income there is to support the growth of and spreading the music as far and wide as possible. Which should be the goal at the end of the day and also benefits all involved.

I'm providing these scenarios as over the past few years, I've seen new producers who received their full cash rates to work with artists who have significant fanbases asking for anywhere from 25 to 50 percent of the master plus upwards of 50% publishing on songs they didn't write on. The "argument" here is that there is less money in music now, which is why those involved in recording should get more than in the past. This is odd to me for a few reasons. First, there are more opportunities to create and collect on music than ever before. Were all of these producers constantly being hired by labels in the pre-digital era and working full time? Probably not, since some producers were too young or not even alive yet in the pre-digital era. Experienced producers that worked all of the time in the pre-digital era should have that many more musicians to work with in the modern era, now that all artists have access to music distribution. I get that that means experienced producers might have to work with more artists to receive the same amount of income than in the pre-digital era. Trust me, I get that this is work. But it's also reality, and complaining doesn't change anything. Not to mention that in the pre-digital era, many producers griped about labels' control and how promotion was handled. So let's try to keep attitudes positive and in perspective, as otherwise we're just going in circles.

Know that I do respect producers. I wouldn't manage them if that weren't the case. But this is an area where my team and I, as well as the attorneys we work with, are seeing artists being asked to give up a lot lately, and we want what is fair and just for all—including producers.

There can also be happy medium. Maybe you can afford only half of a producer's cash rate. In that instance, I'm totally fine with you doubling their producer points, as discussed above. To me, that's a great opportunity that comes out of the modern music industry—we can offer more than the industry's traditional standard points when there isn't a ton of cash up front. However, that doesn't mean you need to sign your life away to a producer.

A similar approach can be taken for studio engineers. Though most engineers just have a rate, and I rarely see them go after a ton of points on a master, if at all. So know that this is an option to propose to them, if it's something they haven't thought of or brought up. However, I am talking about recording engineers. Mixers are starting to ask for more points lately, and you should take the same approach that you took with your producer. A mixer's rates have enormous range from $100 per track to $20,000 a song. Regardless, they are traditionally entitled to one point, or 1 percent of the master recording's revenue.

We will talk about mastering more in depth in the following chapter, but these rates can range from $300 to $3,000, with plenty in between. Mastering engineers do not generally receive points on recordings, but if you're paying someone, you'll want them to sign a work for hire agreement, which we'll outline next. We'll also discuss mastering options on your own in the following chapter. However, I wanted to address the business affairs portion of mastering first, so you are fully covered before you enter the studio.

This all said, make sure anyone you are rewarding points to knows when they will receive these payments. Be it 30 days following each quarter, every 6 months, or annually. And make sure you pay everyone what they're owed for their points and work. If you have the funds to do legal agreements to lay these terms out, that is ideal. But if not, please put down in writing or an email what you and each person working on the recording has agreed to. If doing this via email, make sure each party responds accordingly and agrees to what has been discussed. If you are sent an agreement by your producer, one of your engineers, or anyone on your recording team, I highly recommend having a music attorney review it.

Put a Ring, or a WFH, on It

In *all* of the above conversations, let your players, producer, and engineers know that you'll be sending them a "work for hire" to sign for their payment. This is completely standard and states that you and your band/ group, or whomever is paying for any and all upfront recording costs, own the master in perpetuity. It also outlines that you wrote the songs, or states any previously agreed upon songwriting splits, which we'll discuss in more detail next. I've never *not* had someone sign a work for hire, or

WFH, so if someone has an issue with doing so, to me this is a red flag that the person might cause difficulties in working together moving forward. LegalZoom.com currently offers work for hire agreements for fifty-nine dollars, and I do feel that this is worth investing in. Cosynd.com is another option; their WFH's are $49.99 as of this writing. (Or, you didn't hear it from me, but you can find a generic WFH online and use that.)

Once your recording team signs the work for hire, they can then be paid. Do *not* pay them in full until they sign your work for hire. Otherwise this paperwork tends to become less of a priority for people and signing can be dragged out, or worse, never get done at all. Similarly, when there is cash involved, pay everyone half of their fee up front as a sign of good faith and the balance when they return your signed work for hire and recording has finished. Technically your producer should be having everyone on the recording sign work for hires, but some do not know this. As it is your recording, ensuring such paperwork is taken care of ultimately is on you as the artist at the end of the day. Also make sure that your producer delivers instrumental recordings, if possible based on the recording process, before you make their final payment when they sign your work for hire.

Real Songwriting Splits

Finally, *before* you go into the studio, have a conversation with everyone involved in the recording process on how you're going to handle songwriting. This is the case whether you're a band/group or a solo act, and you *must* have this conversation with your producer and engineers up front. I'm grateful to work with some career songwriters who can ask for whatever splits they want on tracks they co-write. And you know what? They don't ask for "whatever they want" or command higher songwriting splits because of their names. They ask for the percentage that they wrote on the song, be it 5 percent, 50 percent, 90 percent, or whatever the songwriters agree to. Some established artists and songwriters certainly do ask for a higher share of songwriting than what they actually contributed to, and that's fine. Other songwriters go into a collaboration pre-agreeing to a 50/50 split, which I get too. Again, I'm incredibly lucky to have worked with successful songwriters who don't go with either of these routes, and I tend to agree with this. Songwriting splits, in my opinion, should be the actual splits as that is what is fair. If you're writing a song for a massive artist or pop star, it makes sense that they may receive a larger publishing share than what they wrote on the song, if at all. In reality, that is a rare circumstance, but I would be remiss to not mention it here.

With all of this in mind, you need to get together before you commence recording to let everyone involved know that if they feel they write on something, then they need to speak up in the moment or immediately after that session is done. You then need to put the agreed upon splits in writing, often known as a split sheet, or put the agreed upon splits into an email where all parties respond to confirm the agreed upon splits. Coming back months later and demanding credit for writing on a song is both amateur and unprofessional. It can also hold up the release of a recording. If the dispute cannot be settled, you can also submit your own splits to your performing rights organization in protest. Luckily, I've never personally had that happen. But when it does, it's a shame, as the whole point of this is to create art, work together, and move forward. Therefore, have this conversation up front before you begin recording with any and everyone who will even set foot in the studio. And please know that *arranging* or *remixing* is *not* songwriting. This is something I learned as a child in music lessons and in music school long before I was a music professional, and I am surprised when musicians and producers do not know this.

I recommend that you all talk about this up front as a group (i.e., you, the players/full band/group, producer, and engineers). That way no one feels singled out, and everyone is on the same page before recording. The same goes for work for hires. If you let any one into the studio, have them sign a work for hire. All too often, especially when the music takes off, suddenly there are claims that someone who stopped by wrote this lyric or that hook.

Similarly, if you have co-writers, ask if they are OK with their songwriting share being "pre-cleared" for synch. Make sure this clearance is noted in your split sheet or in the email where all parties confirm agreed upon songwriting splits. When there is interest in a song for synchronization rights, all songwriters (or their publisher, but even publishers who tend to own these songwriting rights will generally ask for the writer's blessing), must give their OK for it to move forward. Hence, you don't want to lose a placement because your co-writer is away and off devices. If that happens, the opportunity might go to another song that is easier to clear. I rarely see co-writers not agree to this, as they tend to want their music to be placed. But get it down in writing now, so you don't lose a synch placement in the future.

That said, if one of your co-writers is signed to a major publisher, their publisher may not allow their co-writes to be pre-cleared for synch placements. Hopefully you do not run into such a scenario. However, I know of a synch that was recently landed with a co-writer whose major publisher would not allow the track to be pre-cleared, or cleared at all. Thus, know that a songwriter signed to a major publisher may not be able to grant you this preclearance. If that is the case, encourage your co-writer signed to a major publisher to check out chapter 5 of this book. As that way they can learn how to increase the chances of your co-write being a priority for their publisher to see if any synchs can be landed via the major publisher.

Synchs = Master Recording Revenue Too

Let me add—even though there will be more information on this topic in chapter 5—that everyone who has points on the master recording will be compensated when synch placements are landed. This is because we've discussed points for everyone on the master, unless you are a solo artist who paid hired musicians their full cash rates and therefore does not need to share points on the master. Sadly, although I don't feel that publishing is confusing and will explain to you why in chapter 5, I think some people are confused as to where synch revenue comes from. It seems the thinking is that if they score a cut on publishing, they'll be paid when synchs happen. If those involved—band members, producers, etc.—are receiving points on the master recording, then they will be paid when synch placements are landed. I often hear from non-industry people that "publishing is where the money is" in music. Sure, if you're a great songwriter. Just as there are ways to make money if you are a great recording artist or a killer live performer. It's not that I'm trying to protect some magical holy grail by preserving a songwriter's publishing. It's that I feel everyone should get their fair share. If you write on a song, you get a cut. If you didn't, you don't. And again, if you are a player or producer or engineer who is not receiving your full cash rate, you are absolutely entitled to more points than usual on the master recording. I would be remiss to not add that yes, there is a little more money on the publishing "side" when synch placements are landed, due to performing rights organization, or PRO payments. Instead of going after publishing on songs one didn't write on, I encourage all of us to support the bi-partisan "Ask Musicians For Music (AM-FM) Act," which was introduced in 2019. Should the act pass, it would then offer recording artists in the U.S. similar royalties as to what songwriters receive from their PRO's, except this time on the master recording side.

Remixes and Arranging

If you are doing a remix or want a new arrangement for a song, these are more often than not, flat fees payments. Remixers should absolutely sign a work for hire, and for good measure, I recommend doing so with an arranger as well. As you've learned, if there is truly no cash, you can get creative with points on the master recording if the remixer and arranger agree to do so. I would keep both around 5 points or less in a no cash situation, and 2.5 points if they're receiving half of their rate when working with a limited budget. That said, if a massive artist is remixing your song, they understandably might ask for more points on the remix, as their name alone will help the track with exposure. Regardless, I'd like for you to in the least retain 50% of your master recording royalties when working with a "name" remixer.

Releasing Cover Songs

If you are planning on releasing any cover songs, you will need to estimate your sales and streaming numbers for these songs and pre-pay for what is called a mechanical license from The Harry Fox Agency. This can generally be obtained from Harry Fox's website at harryfox.com and HFA's site also provides rate charts to help you with this.If you happen to be releasing a cover song by songwriters who are not covered by Harry Fox, that writer(s)' publisher likely has a portal where you can pre-pay for this license. If the songwriter doesn't have a publisher, then you can reach out to the writer directly to pay the current statutory rate of 9.1 cents USD per song sold, divided pro rata between all writers/publishers of the song.

Group/Band Agreements

This is also a good time to get a band/group agreement together. I'd like you to split ownership of the master recording equally. As, again, if different band members contribute to songwriting, that is handled in a fair manner with the songwriting splits on the publishing side of the music you have created. If one person in the group is fronting all recording costs, I feel that person should own the master and cut in band members on master recording points as musicians. If some group members are paying for the recording, they own the master, while the others will be entitled to a percentage of the master royalties after expenses are recouped. Those who paid for the recording then retain ownership of the master recordings.

Also decide how you want to handle income beyond your recordings. If one or more than one member of a group/band is paying for everything surrounding live appearances, I'd argue that they're entitled to being paid back for each show/tour's expenses, with the net income (a.k.a. what's left after the funder has been paid back) being split equally from there. Same for merchandise, if one person is fronting the costs. If everyone is able to chip in, everyone splits all income equally right away, as you are all entitled to the funds as they come in to recoup your investment and profit from. I feel that all other revenue streams—branding, sponsorship, etc.—that don't have up front expenses should be split equally amongst band/group members. Ideally, you want all of this reflected in a legal band agreement. If that isn't in the financial cards, at least put it in an email after discussing what everyone has agreed to, so you have it down in writing.

CHAPTER 4:

HOW TO RECORD WITH OR WITHOUT A BUDGET

N ow it's time to get into the fun stuff—recording! As mentioned, one of the major game changers from the brick-and-mortar music industry is that artists can now record for much less than what it cost in the analog era. And if you want to record to tape, awesome! That is certainly a sound that appeals to some, and I understand that. But for now, we're going to assume you are recording digitally.

Let me make it clear that I'm making an assumption that you have access to a smartphone and ideally a computer. If these are items you do not have, ask around. I'm going to bet that someone will let you use either or both to get going. Either way, this chapter was written with my friend Bobby Lord. Bobby has worked with musicians in some of the biggest bands in the world, made music on his own, and does so every day at a podcast network, composing and recording music when necessary. Bobby has a perfect mix of experience, as he knows how to record on the cheap as well as in world-class situations. Here we go!

Smartphone Demos

It's easy to forget, but those who have a smartphone are carrying around a microphone and computer in their pocket. This can be a great way to begin not only to learn how to record, but also a simple way to put down any songwriting ideas whenever they arise—assuming you have your phone on you. Here are a variety of apps to get you rolling:

- Voice Memos: Voice Memos is an app that is already built into iPhones with a variety of equivalent free apps available for Android. You might already use this in your daily life, but either way this is a great app to put down ideas while you're on the go, so you can refer to them later. And if you wake up in the middle of the night with an incredible idea, create a Voice Memo so you remember it in the morning! The quality of the recording isn't enough to result in a super high-fidelity professional recording, but that said, an experienced mixer may be able to make it work for a track, podcasts, or other use under the right circumstances. And it depends on what you're going for. Maybe you love the low-fi sound of Voice Memos. For example, Sufjan Stevens has released music recorded on his iPhone for an outtakes and demos album.

- Spire: iZotope has a free multitrack recording app for iPhone and Android called Spire. The app also works in conjunction with their Spire recording interface.

- Keezy: Programs such as Keezy, which is also free, are tactile and simple samplers that you can use to brainstorm ideas and record them onto your phone. You can also later record these into a digital audio workstation, or DAW, on a computer.

Recording with a Laptop

As mentioned, we're assuming you have access to your own laptop or a friend's laptop to record your music. And if you are creating remixes, mixing music, or working on EDM (electronic dance music) or something similar, it's actually possible to do it all without a recording interface by using just your laptop, a digital audio workstation (DAW), and decent quality headphones that we'll recommend below.

The industry standard DAW is ProTools ($599 USD, plus $99/year), but Logic Pro ($200), Ableton ($749), Audition ($252), Reaper ($60 to $225), and more are also great options. All prices throughout this chapter and book are as of this writing.

Like so many other things, YouTube is a great place for free tutorials, but, viewer beware, as there are also not-great options on YouTube. Here are a few we recommend to get rolling:

- Tutorials for beginners: www.youtube.com/user/ recordingrevolution

- Pensado's Place: A classic internet show where different mixers talk about their philosophies/history, and Dave Pensado does little tutorials in each episode: www.youtube.com/user/PensadosPlace

- Plugins: If you want to learn the specifics of plugins, Fabfilter makes great plugins, and they also make amazing tutorials, such as this: https://youtu.be/IDMrLQGd21w

Headphones/Monitor Speakers

It is likely you're in a situation where headphones will be more suitable than monitor speakers—say, if you have neighbors or are working from a coffee shop. There is a wide range of great options for headphones. Here are some that we recommend:

- AKG K240 Studio Semi-open ($69)

- Sennheiser HD 280 Pro Closed-back ($99)

- Audio-Technica ATH-M50x Closed-back ($149)

- Sennheiser HD 600 Open-back Audiophile/professional head-phones ($399). This is a more expensive option for those looking for industry-standard, high-quality pro mixing headphones.

Earbuds and AirPods can also be mixed on, but these lack the bass-response and fidelity needed for recording and mixing decisions. Considering most AirPods cost well over $100, you're better off grabbing a pair of the headphones mentioned above for recording purposes. But AirPods and earbuds can be valuable to reference what your music will sound like to most people otherwise.

If you do have access to a soundproof or remote space, the KRK Rokit ($150) and Yamaha HS monitor speakers ($200 plus) are solid and popular entry-level monitors.

Recording Interface

If you want to record an acoustic instrument (e.g., your voice, acoustic guitar, etc.), you'll need a microphone. To get the microphone signal into your DAW on your laptop, you'll need a recording interface. You'll also need an interface if you want to get a guitar or synthesizer signal into your DAW. There are a variety of types and styles of interfaces, so you'll want to consider a few elements:

- How many sources/microphones will you need to record simulta-neously?: If you're recording a podcast with four people speak-ing, you'll need four mics and therefore, an interface that can handle four inputs. In audio, there are a myriad of ways to achieve any given task. So while it's technically true that you could record four microphones and use a mixer to mix those signals down to a single output (meaning you could use an interface that only has one input, such as the Apogee One for $275), you would lose the ability to have each of those signals on their own track. Modern interfaces are cheap enough, so an interface with four preamps and enough inputs and outputs, or I/O, are not prohibitively expensive.

- <u>What can your computer use?</u>: Interfaces connect with computers via USB 2 and 3, Thunderbolt, and Firewire (for older computers). USB 3 and Thunderbolt will be faster than the older connection types, but that doesn't mean the older connections can't still be optimized and useful. Again, there is a ton of knowledge on audio forums about this throughout the web, and as always, Google is your friend here.

- <u>What is your budget?</u>: This seems like it may go without saying, but there is a massive range of prices for interfaces, with many being prohibitive for most people. If you're just getting going and want to record your own songs, a cheaper interface like Focusrite Scarlett Solo ($110 plus) could potentially be just fine. But if you're trying to make an investment for the long-term and want to mix at a professional level, you may want to look into something like Universal Audio Apollo Twin ($600 plus) or x8p ($2,500 plus), if possible.

Microphones

You may be beginning to sense a pattern here, as similar to any sort of gear—as with many things in audio—there's an enormous price range when it comes to microphones, or mics, as well as a wide range of considerations for what type of mic to use. That being said, there are plenty of great entry-level microphones that you can now buy for relatively reasonable prices. And as you probably know, used options for any sort of gear are available, but check ratings and previous use before buying. In the meantime, here are some options for mics that we recommend:

- <u>Shure SM57 ($99)</u>: One of the most famous microphones of all time, with a reputation for being a versatile workhorse. If you can afford one mic for your home studio, this should be it.

- <u>Rode NT1 ($269)</u>: This is a great-bang-for-your-buck microphone, delivering sound quality high above its price point.

- <u>Warm Audio Mics (range of prices)</u>: Warm Audio is a small, Texas-based company that makes affordable replicas of famous and more expensive microphones.

- <u>Shure SM7 ($399), ElectroVoice RE20 ($450), and Neumann U87 ($2,200 plus)</u>: These are examples of famous broadcast microphones used in many radio stations. Any of these would be great for any podcast, as well as for recording a singing voice or acoustic instrument. These are going to be your more expensive mic options.

Mixing

Mixing is a series of different techniques to "mix together" a bunch of different elements into one finished piece. Again, let's set aside mastering, because as time goes on, mastering gets more and more conflated with mixing, for good reason. But in its simplest explanation, mixing is all about volumes, levels, and loudness. However, engineers use many different tools to affect volumes in different ways, and that's the key. They don't only use faders (i.e., tools in a DAW that control volume) to mix, but they use many tools like equalization (which is filtering that affects the *volume* of a specific/controlled part of the audible frequency spectrum), compression/expansion (which is processing that affects the dynamic range of a given audio source, which again has to do with volume), and many other creative tools such as reverb, delay, distortion, stereo imaging processing, etc., etc., etc. Yet in some essence, every single one of these tools is affecting volume in some way. The discipline of "mixing" is learning techniques, both technical and creative, for affecting these many different types of volume in ways that achieve a "mix" that is satisfying in a technical manner (i.e., it doesn't distort your stereo, doesn't have too much bass or treble, doesn't wildly fluctuate in volume) and in creative ways that "sound cool!" (e.g., that distortion on the vocal "sounds cool," that reverb "sounds cool!")

When it comes time to mix your music, you have a few elements to consider. What kind of mix are you going for? Who is your audience? If you're aiming for a more polished radio sound, you might want to save up and hire a professional mixing engineer who has experience using the sophisticated techniques it can take to achieve such a sound.

But it's not always necessary to take this approach. Maybe you're going for something lo-fi in the vein of Liz Phair, Snail Mail, Guided By Voices, etc. Plenty of musicians are able to use instinct and unusual, creative approaches to achieve really unique and special mixes. Oftentimes, those very instincts aid artists in their careers, allowing them to carve out unique sounds for themselves. The specialness of such mixes can sometimes be compromised by a more traditional, or "slick," radio mix.

Like so much in art and music, mixing is an inherently subjective discipline, and there's an infinite amount of ways to creatively mix. Again, YouTube is a goldmine for mixing tutorials, as are magazines such as *TapeOp*. People often think there is a "correct" way to mix. While there are definite rules and best practices in audio that can help achieve certain sounds or minimize unwanted sounds (e.g., unwanted distortion, phase problems, etc., etc., etc.), there's no "right" philosophy to mixing. Just as there isn't any sort of "right" way to create music.

With that in mind, we'll break down options for mixing no matter your budget:

- Mixing without a budget: If you do not have a budget for mixing, consider mixing your music yourself! Watch as many online tutorials as you have time for, and follow your inner creative spirit. Or reach out to a friend who is trained in mixing to see if they'll work with you on honing your skills.

- <u>Mixing with some sort of a budget</u>: We've discussed much of this in the previous chapter, but you can also pay a friend who is savvy at mixing. Paying a friend will allow them to prioritize your project and incentivize them to put real time into the mix.

- <u>Mixing if you have extra cash</u>: Consider finding a recording studio and hiring a staff engineer there to mix your music. They may have the experience and gear necessary to get a polished sound for your music, if that is what you are going for.

Mastering

Mastering is an often-misunderstood part of mixing. It typically refers to processing done to the final stereo mix of a given piece of music. But today's practices have blended mixing and mastering so much that they've become, at times, indistinguishable from each other. And to be clear, that sentence is from Bobby, not Emily! To some, mastering simply translates to "making music as loud and bright as radio music so I can compete," and this truly may be all you want to do with your mix. Regardless, here are some options for mastering to complete what you have in mind:

- <u>No/Small Budget</u>: Websites such as LANDR (nine to nineteen dollars) or Auphonic (a site for podcasting that is free to eighty-nine dollars) offer auto-mastering that will get your recordings to levels that will be "loud" enough and competitive with what else is out there.

- <u>With a budget</u>: You can hire a mastering engineer whose entire job is to completely polish, finesse, and possibly "fix" your final mix. These are deeply experienced engineers who have acoustically treated rooms, high-level monitoring gear, and the proper knowledge to know what to listen for when mastering your music. They often have rooms where they can hear things that you cannot (often in the low-end bass and super-high-end treble) and address problems in your mix that you didn't even know you had. They can also apply processing to your recordings in ways that automated systems just currently cannot. Going a route like this can cost anywhere from $300 to $3,000. When deciding what to spend on mastering, consider the following:

- <u>Where will the music be heard?</u>: If you're doing SoundCloud demos before a full-on proper release, you probably do not need to spend thousands of dollars on mastering.

- <u>Are you happy with how the music sounds already?</u>: Does it already sound comparable to a certain track or sound that you referenced in recording or what you are going for? If that's the case, you seriously may not need mastering! Listen to your gut instinct to decide if you're mastering just because you think you need to.

Home Studio versus Hiring a Traditional Recording Studio

With all of the above taken into consideration, here is information on the differences between recording on your own or hiring a "traditional" recording studio. Ironically, many pro studios are home studios, but we'll break it down so you can make an informed choice.

There are a few differences between doing all of this on your own and hiring professionals. A professional will likely be aware of problems your music may have that even you are not aware of. If a professional has an acoustically treated room and massive, high-quality monitor speakers, they may hear enormous, bloated low end that you couldn't detect on tiny earbuds. Only after detecting problems like that can you fix them. Or maybe, your music has distortion problems that you just can't figure out, and a pro can track down where in the signal chain the distortion is occurring. Maybe the aesthetic of your music requires Autotune, and the pro knows how to use that software. Maybe your mix is *incredible* based on instinct alone, but the overall loudness is too high and distorts on some but not *all* playback systems (and therefore, you didn't detect it previously). A professional can help detect such problems to ensure your music will play back in high quality across as many systems as possible. In other words, they have the experience, knowledge, software, and additional gear to make sure your music sounds great whether it's played on $2,000 studio speakers, Beats by Dre, AirPods, or laptop speakers.

Regardless, even professionals agree that the more you can learn and do on your own, the more money you'll save on studio time. So it's in every musician's best interest to learn and grow their recording skills as much as possible.

Engaging While Recording

If you need to hole up and completely block off the outside world, I totally get this. Try writing a book when I'm currently on a relatively remote island, with my phone on silent, and *still* get interrupted by neighbors, construction workers, a butt dial from my parents, and iMessage on my computer. It's nearly impossible to get still and quiet in our modern world to truly focus. That all said, hopefully whatever studio situation you set up becomes some sort of temporary sanctuary for your art. So take this next piece of advice with a grain of salt: if it speaks to you, consider keeping your fans in the loop while recording. You don't need to give away the farm, just some sort of teaser and engagement with the audience so they are part of your journey and excited for what is to come. For some, this is natural. If this truly sounds like hell on earth to you, snap a photo of yourself and those who worked on the music in the studio the day that you wrap and share that. Your social media and Patreon accounts are already set up, so this should be relatively easy to do, no matter how much or little you feel like sharing at this stage.

A Note on Artwork

While immersed in the recording process, *do not* forget about artwork! I've worked with artists releasing music when it is far from their first rodeo and they *still* forget about artwork until the last minute. Try to avoid this stress by thinking about what you might want to do for single/album/EP/whatever artwork *before* you enter the studio. You don't have to make any final decisions, but at least the seed has been planted in your mind. When you are in the mixing and definitely the mastering stage, that is a perfect time to decide on and finalize your artwork. Similarly, if someone else does your artwork or it is a photograph, make sure they sign a work for hire. Such artwork often holds up releases at the highest of levels, which creates unnecessary stress for all. Get in the habit of getting ahead of your release with an artwork plan so it's a creative and fun part of the process, instead of something that you just rush out and that is unnecessarily laborious.

CHAPTER 5:

MUSIC PUBLISHING ISN'T SCARY OR CONFUSING + HOW TO LAND A SYNCH PLACEMENT

Congratulations! Your recordings are wrapped up. Or at least, headed to mastering. Now we'll discuss a topic that has sent fear into the bones of countless musicians *and* music industry professionals: publishing.

I understand why publishing gets an intimidating wrap. Years ago, music publishing companies would sign away an artist's songwriting rights for life. For example, I was on a panel once with the Village People's current manager. The topic of publishing came up, and I said, "I'm guessing that if any members of the Village People wrote 'YMCA,' they don't own the music publishing rights to it." I was correct, and there are many stories of such instances where a songwriter signs their rights away for what sounds like a good chunk of money—say $10,000 to $25,000 in the 1970s—but the publishing rights went on to make millions.

Similar to how the modern music industry cracked recording and distribution wide open for all to access, the same mechanisms and access now exists for all songwriters in music publishing.

What Is Music Publishing?

But first, what *is* music publishing? It's quite simple. Do you know what a record company does, in theory? I've never met anyone who can't answer the second question, let alone a musician. Artists often grow up dreaming of being on specific labels. They know that a record company's job is to promote, and in the legal sense of the term, exploit their recordings for maximum financial gain.

A publisher is the *exact* same concept for your songwriting! A music publisher's job, at its core, is to go out and collect money for every use of your song. It is also their job to find as much work for that song as possible, often in the form of "synch," or synchronization placements. They additionally set up co-writing sessions or songwriting for other artists, if that is something you desire. As discussed, a synch placement is the use of music in a film, TV/web show, or commercial/advert. Certainly labels and unsigned artists are also going after synchs because, as mentioned, those who own and share in percentage points on the master recording will also be compensated.

That's it! There is *no* need to be so terrified and run to the hills with confusion regarding the concept of music publishing. If that has been your mindset, know that you're not alone. I'm constantly shocked when industry professionals, who are often older than me and have decades of experience say, "Yeah, I never understood that whole publishing thing." This is both mind-boggling and sad to me. If you're going to enter a field, in this instance music, don't you want to know everything about how it works? But that's neither here nor there. Let's get you set up and organized so you know how to collect revenue on your songwriting via music publishing forever.

ASCAP/BMI/SESAC—a.k.a. Performing Rights Organizations or PRO's

If you are based in the United States, pick a performing rights society to sign up with. Your PRO will collect public performance royalties for your songwriting not limited to music played on the radio, for broadcast, and for its use in any physical public setting such as a venue, shop, airport, or dining establishment. The vast majority of songwriters are with ASCAP (The American Society of Composers, Authors, and Publishers) or BMI (Broadcast Music Inc.). A smaller amount of songwriters are signed up with SESAC (initially named for the Society of European Stage Authors and Composers) and GMR (Global Music Rights), though these PRO's are currently invite only. It technically does not make a difference which performing rights organization you go with—they are all supposed to be the same. However, I would be remiss to not mention Zoë Keating's excellent point in this book's Foreword on doing some research based on what kind of music you make. That is an awesome tip. But know that if you truly do not have the time or interest that going with one society or another isn't going to make a massive difference on moving your career forward, if at all. If you are able to research which society might be the most appropriate fit for your music, great. If you're already signed up, Zoë Keating also shared with me during our conversation that changing societies is a total pain. My point? Don't overthink which society you are going with unless you want to.

If you are based in the UK, you're going to want to sign up with Performing Rights Society (PRS). If in France, sign up with the Society of Authors, Composers and Publishers of Music, or SACEM. A full global list to find the performing rights societies in your country can be found here: https://en.wikipedia.org/wiki/List_of_copyright_collection_societies.

The only slight reason, beyond what type of music you make, to decide on which society to go with so it might give you an opportunity once in awhile, is if you know someone at one of the aforementioned performing rights societies. If so, I recommend going with them. All PRO's do e-blasts on their songwriters and showcases at industry conferences and festivals. Give yourself the best shot to land these opportunities by trying to connect with a human at your society. If not, do not fret, as literally every songwriter in the world has signed up for a PRO, and realistically there are only so many promotional and live slots to go around. That said, it's nice to have a human there no matter what for when questions or concerns on your collections do arise. All PRO's have customer service, but who doesn't prefer having a real connection? However, again, if you do not know someone at your PRO yet, that's OK. Doing so won't necessarily make or break one's career by any means.

Setlist Submissions for PRO's.

Some PRO's, such as BMI in the US and PRS in the UK, accept setlist submissions from artists' live performances to calculate royalties more accurately. Others use formulas to parse out royalties accordingly to the songwriters they are collecting for. As more PRO's are accepting setlists directly from artists as time evolves, ask if yours does. And if so, make sure you regularly turn in your setlists from your shows to your PRO.

Only Sign Up for ASCAP, BMI, SESAC, or any PRO as a Songwriter Once

The subheading above says it all. Once you are with one performing rights organization, you cannot go and sign up for another one for your next release. Even if you could, you'd just be convoluting your own revenue streams, and are under contract until your term with your current PRO expires. Similarly, you are one songwriter. Don't try and register with a different performing rights society as a songwriter again just because you formed a new band, group, or changed your stage name. I want to make clear that you sign up for a single PRO, as a songwriter. Then register your individual songs as the works are created and all songwriters have agreed to the splits in writing.

When you initially sign up, you'll have the option to create your own publishing name or designee, which is separate from you as an individual songwriter. Because, just to make things more confusing for everyone, your songwriting is split fifty/fifty between a "writer's share" and a "publisher's share." If you do not have a publishing company collecting songwriting revenue on your behalf—which is totally fine and we'll talk about next in this chapter—you therefore own your share of royalties as a songwriter, as well as your publishing name's share. So you'll see on a PRO statement for a song you 100 percent wrote that 50 percent is collected by the PRO for you as a songwriter, and the other 50 percent is collected on for the publishing designee you created. You also don't have to create a publishing designee at all. So feel free to just register and sign up with your name, as that can help to keep things streamlined when reviewing your statements.

At this stage in the methodical order we're teaching you, you've now recorded your new music and know the songwriting splits. Now it's time to get each song registered with your PRO account. Moving forward, do this every time you finish a song and agree to the songwriting splits, if there are any, with co-writers. Always put any songwriting splits that you agree to down in writing with your co-writers so there is a record of it.

Collecting on Your Publishing/Publishing Deals

If you are signed up and have registered all of your songs with your PRO, and your songs are getting covered, sold, streamed and more - *you're still not set up to collect all funds owed to you for your songwriting.*

Back in the day, a songwriter would have had to sign with a music publisher to collect on their publishing, which encompasses a variety of songwriting revenue streams within publishing. As mentioned, many of these deals in the twentieth century—which sadly but rarely still get offered to songwriters once in a while—meant artists were signing their songwriting rights away forever for a nominal sum. The great news is that now there are a variety of deal structures and options that allow artists to collect their publishing royalties that don't force them to sign their songwriting rights away. But you also don't have to sign with a publishing company to collect your publishing royalties at all in the modern era if you don't want to. Not that there's anything wrong with publishing companies! Because, as mentioned, most publishing companies in the modern era will now offer you deals where you can continue to own and control your songwriting copyrights long-term. As follows, let's break down your options on how to collect revenue on your music publishing.

Songtrust

If you are a brand-new songwriter and just getting going, sign up for Songtrust immediately. I have nothing to gain by encouraging this. Songtrust was founded by the principals at Downtown Music Publishing, who are forward-thinking and therefore have essentially democratized music publishing collection for all. This is similar to how you can distribute your music worldwide in the modern era (the latter of which we'll discuss in the next chapter). Songtrust uses Downtown's world-class music publishing collection system to collect on behalf of any songwriter who wants to work with them. There is a $100 fee to get going, but I do recommend them over others, as I know what a great job the Downtown / Songtrust team does in finding every single penny for songwriters. They do retain 15 percent, which is standard for the next level of publishing deal—called "administrative" or "admin" deals—that we'll discuss shortly. Therefore, you retain 85 percent of your royalties, as well as own your copyrights, and can leave at any time after a year. Again, what I think is brilliant about Songtrust is that everyone has access to music publishing collection, instead of just songwriters who have access to a publishing deal, which was the case in the past.

Note that Songtrust does *not* pitch your music for synch placements, but we'll talk about options to do so later in this chapter.

<u>CD Baby/Tunecore Publishing Administration</u>
We're going to talk about a variety of distribution options in the next chapter, including CD Baby and Tunecore. Maybe you've heard of or used these services for music distribution already. They're both solid companies for what they do. However, they also have a simple box that feels like a no-brainer to check. Currently this is advertised on CD Baby's site as "Make more money with music publishing." On Tunecore the headline reads "The songs you wrote might be earning money you don't even know about. We can find and collect it for you." Who wouldn't check that box? And although I'm not saying these are bad or ill intended companies, when songwriters check said box when signing up for their music distribution, they've just committed their publishing administration for the music they're distributing, often without much thought.

This came up recently with a national act I began managing. I was shocked when she told me her publishing revenue wasn't currently collected by anyone. We decided that Songtrust was the way to go for her. I asked if she had ever checked a box with CD Baby or Tunecore regarding her publishing while distributing a record and was told no. Months later, we received an alert from Tunecore asking to update some information. No big deal. When I updated her information from a previous album that I wasn't involved in, lo and behold, Tunecore had been collecting on her publishing. Our team is now untangling this as we speak. As we had registered the songs with Songtrust and are now spending time on the aforementioned untangling, which cuts into time we'd otherwise be spending moving her career forward. By all means, it's literally our job to get this all organized. But that's why I'm telling you *not* to check the publishing administration boxes with CD Baby and Tunecore when distributing music. If you want, you totally can! I just recommend that all of your publishing administration is in one place for your ease of collecting funds instead of getting one album's publishing money here and another release's publishing money there. Also know that Songtrust is the backend for CD Baby's publishing administration, and CD Baby charges a slightly higher cash fee per release to access this administration. So you might as well go straight to the source and save a few bucks over time.

"Admin" or Administrative Deals

If you do have the opportunity to work with a publishing company, great. There are a variety of deal structures available, but we're going to talk about the two most common that are out there. First up is an "admin" or administrative deal. As mentioned, this is *very* similar to Songtrust's terms, but there isn't a $100 up-front fee involved. You will control and retain all copyrights and are essentially licensing your songwriting rights to a company to collect on your songwriting on your behalf. These deals are generally eighty-five/fifteen percent, eighty/twenty percent, or seventy-five/twenty-five percent in the songwriter's favor. I don't recommend going below 75 percent. By all means, all of these deals are negotiable. You could go for retaining a higher percentage and agree to a longer term for the deal. And with anything, as your career grows and your songwriting makes more money, you will in turn gain leverage for such negotiations. Advances, or advance payments to songwriters, do happen in administrative deals.

But they will be lower than what you will receive in a co-publishing deal, which we'll discuss next. Thus, if you're getting an advance on an admin deal, you can negotiate your collection rate based on a lower or higher advance. Advances don't always happen in admin deals, so don't be offended if you're a brand-new artist without a track record and aren't able to get one.

"Co-pub" or Co-publishing Deals

The other main type of publishing deal is a co-publishing, or "co-pub," deal. In this instance, the publisher will retain a portion or all of your songwriting copyright for a set amount of time or even forever—also known as perpetuity. Believe it or not, I'm not opposed to this, depending on the situation. When looking at all of an artist's revenue streams/rights, I have seen some artists give up a portion of their publishing rights for large advances. This can help a new and developing artist fund promotion and touring costs to continue to grow their careers. In other instances, I've seen artists buy their home with a publishing advance. So it's up to you. Getting a solid amount of cash up front can absolutely benefit an artist personally and professionally, especially in a world where record company advances are inconsistent at best—if you want or have access to working with a label.

Working Your Publishing Deal

If you've scored a publishing deal, congratulations! Now it's time to get to work. This might be a surprise, as you've just met someone or a team of people who have told you how much they believe in you and your songwriting. And they do! They wouldn't be working with you otherwise. However, most publishing companies have literally thousands of songs they are working with, and we want yours to stand out.

Even if you are one of the greatest songwriters in history, don't you want your music to be as much of a priority as possible? To do just that, put yourself in your publisher's shoes. How can you make their job as seamless as possible? We're going to talk about synchs next, but for now, one reason publishers tend to like working with me (besides that as a fan and professional, I am drawn to working with strong songwriters) is that we do a great job of keeping our publishers informed and in the loop.

To do so, again, make sure you have connected with as many human beings at your publishing company as possible. You obviously don't want to email them every day, on weekends, or on holidays. But think about sending an email on a Monday or Tuesday, about once or twice a month, updating them on any highlights you may have. Examples of this helpful information include press hits, tour dates, and reminders that you're happy to put them, music supervisors, or anyone they want on your shows' guest lists. Such a simple and organized gesture is going to help you stand out from the crowd among your fellow songwriters. It will also keep your music at the forefront of your publisher's mind, which is what we want. If you are unable to send such emails at the top of the week, you can utilize programs such as Boomerang for Gmail, which will let you schedule emails to be sent on a day and time of your choosing. This allows you to write such messages on your timetable and schedule, while letting technology send it at a more optimal time to ensure your email is a priority and doesn't get pushed down in the receiver's inbox.

How to Land a Synch

Years ago, I wrote an article called "How to Land a Synch." We *still* receive regular emails from artists thanking me for this information. Of course, we could never guarantee landing a synch placement. But the content of the article explains not only all of the above in this chapter but also teaches you how to put your music in the best possible position to land synch placements, assuming that is a goal.

Instrumentals/Delivery

Most producers know to also deliver instrumental versions of songs, if possible, based on the recording process. But *plenty* still tend to forget, unless you ask. So please ensure that you have WAV files of your instrumentals, as many synch placements are sans vocals.

Similarly, please type up and be ready to deliver all of your lyrics. It is a publisher's and synch pitching company's dream if you can deliver WAV files and high-quality MP3 versions of the songs, WAV and high-quality MP3 versions of your instrumentals, and lyrics, all in one organized email. I've been throwing in Spotify links for ease of listening as well. Each format should be a downloadable link (e.g. a Dropbox link), *not* as files attached to an email. Many folks do not deliver complete or any assets in an organized manner. So make your publisher or synch-pitching person's day while simultaneously making their job, and the work they're doing for you and your music, easier.

Synch Company Options

In the aforementioned "How to Land a Synch" article, I outlined a variety of synch pitching options, whether you have a publishing company pitching your music or not. If you are just getting going and have signed up for Songtrust, these first two options are for you.

- Music Libraries and Re-titling: First up—and I know it kills my friends at publishing companies that I'm suggesting this, but too bad and hear me out—there are synch companies that anyone can upload their music to. The understandable reason this makes music publishers lose their minds is that some of these companies will re-title your works to receive a share of public performance royalties (i.e., funds from ASCAP/BMI/SESAC or your PRO) on their placements. Which definitely isn't ideal. *But* we all have to start somewhere. And either way, read your agreements and the fine print to know what you're signing up for—and when you can get out of it. These types of companies include Jingle Punks and Music Dealers and are available to just about everyone who submits to them. Oftentimes music distributors such as CD Baby will also offer you synch-pitching options. Again, if you're just getting started and have no other options to be pitched to synch, I say go for it. And again, always look up the terms and how quickly you can get out of these deals. You can usually terminate, after giving notice, anywhere from seven days to a year.

But, like anything we're talking about, you want to put yourself in the best position to land placements. So reach out and find a human at these or your synch company of choice. And as mentioned, send them a monthly succinct, organized, bullet-pointed email with your latest and greatest career highlights (e.g., press hits, tour dates, guest list offers, etc.) Also let them know if you're able to come and play at their office to showcase your material for their team if you can, or when you're on tour. Not all of these companies are on the East or West Coasts either. I know plenty of artists that have connected with Music Dealers' team in Chicago, which is smack in the middle of the country.

And before some flip out because I'm suggesting getting rolling with companies that may re-title songs, know that I used that exact strategy when taking on a brand-new artist a few years ago. Through one of these synch companies that has an open submission policy, the band scored a $15,000 synch placement on an ad for a major over-the-counter drug that everyone has heard of. I knew this fee was super low, even though it sounds like a decent amount of cash for a new artist. Also keep in mind these re-titling companies take up to a 50 percent commission, so it's really a $7,500 gross payment, which is also incredibly low for an advertising placement this large. However, the commercial aired, among other times, during the World Series; which is obviously on a major network in prime time. This means that the band/songwriters' BMI royalties went through the roof—i.e., to six-figures—and their iTunes sales spiked. (Plus they owned their master on their own label, so they kept all of the funds from those sales as well. I'm dating myself with the iTunes sales reference from the download era, but you get the idea.) All of this in addition to growing their fanbase by exposing their music to a national audience. Following that, I was then able to negotiate a lucrative publishing deal for the band and wrap up their deal with the re-titling company. You've got to start somewhere.

- Selective Pitching Companies: The next "level" of synch pitching, in my opinion, is working with a selective third-party synch-pitching company, such as Terrorbird, Zync Music, or Bankrobber. These companies do not generally offer open submissions to catalogs. Remember my friend Lauren Ross from chapter 1? She is at Terrorbird, and similar to Lauren, these companies tend to know what they can place. They do not, generally, retain any ownership and receive 20 to 25 percent of synch placements they land. I say generally, as Terrorbird also offers publishing deals, though they do only admin deals, so their songwriters maintain copyright ownership. However, many labels and independent artists work with such companies for synch placements only. You can then collect your songwriting /

publishing royalties through your PRO and companies like Songtrust. More often than not, you can leave these synch companies within a reasonable amount of time, per the terms that you signed up for, by giving notice and without being locked in for the rest of your life.

- Publishing Companies: And finally, as mentioned, an artist can sign an admin or co-pub deal with a publishing company. After you sign either of these deals, that company will then be pitching your songwriting to synch. We've discussed how to make your publisher's days easier and stay in the forefront of their minds. This will help you land synchs when you are signed to a publishing company as well as stand out from the throng of other songwriters that they also publish.

A Note on Exclusivity and Approvals

A situation you don't want to fall into is having everyone and their mother pitching you to synch. Especially at the re-titling level, many companies will allow you to work with them non-exclusively. This sounds awesome in theory! Who wouldn't want as many people pitching your music as possible?

As a young manager, I learned the hard way that this isn't the way to go. The music community is small, and the music supervisor community (the people who decide which songs get placed in the film/show/advert they're working on) is even smaller. In the early days of my career, I had a young band signed up with a slew of non-exclusive synch companies. They were up for a $30,000 synch, but when there was confusion over which company had pitched it first, we lost the placement. No music supervisor wants, or has time, to deal with such a mess. As you can see, if you have a variety of companies pitching your music, this can lead to a synch placement train wreck.

I now prefer to have one company, usually a songwriter's publisher, pitching on the songwriting side with a Terrorbird-esque company pitching on the master side. You can absolutely make these professionals' lives easier by giving one company the authority to pitch both the master and publishing side, as this is a great strategy to land synchs quickly. This is because no music supervisor wants to, or often even can due to deadlines, wait around while everyone gets permission to use the song. I encourage you to go this route, often called "one-stop," if you do not feel you can respond to all inquiries within twenty-four hours. Similarly, remember how we discussed your co-writers signing a waiver that their songwriting share is "pre-cleared" for synch? You need that waiver here in order to not turn off music supervisors, who would otherwise assume that your music will take longer to clear than another song they're considering that might only have a sole songwriter.

My office has a policy of responding to all messages within twenty-four business hours, if not sooner, which is why we're often able to have a publisher represent the publishing side of a song and a selective synch-pitching company handle the master. They know me well enough to have confidence that we'll get back to them in time to ensure we don't lose the synch placement. So figure out which situation makes the most sense for you, but do not have more than two companies pitching the same music, as it's going to hurt you in the long run.

CHAPTER 6:

SETTING UP YOUR RELEASE AND DISTRIBUTION PLAN

It's time to unlock the other major change that has occurred in the music industry over the last century. The first was access to recording tools. The second is giving you, and all musicians, the keys to global distribution.

Direct to Fan Distribution

You are already set up with a "direct to fan" distribution channel, which also means you're obtaining fans' email addresses through CASH Music's tools or your Squarespace website. Now it's time to upload your music to Bandcamp. I've been so pro-Bandcamp in the music industry that some have jokingly accused me of working on Bandcamp's behalf. I'm not. What I love about Bandcamp is that those who own master recording rights, which on Bandcamp are often artists themselves, can upload their music and the rights holder is given the email addresses of fans who purchase their music. This is not the case with any major streaming or download platform such as Spotify or Apple Music.

Additionally, I encourage you to set a minimum price on Bandcamp, but otherwise let fans pay what they want. We did this recently for an artist who released a new song, and the track averaged $8 per fan. In download world, why would we otherwise limit fans to $0.99, if they want to pay more to support you and your work?

Global Digital Distribution Via CD Baby, Tunecore, and Label Engine

Next, let's discuss your options for distribution to major platforms that house catalogs of music including Spotify, Apple Music, Tidal, Amazon Music, YouTube Music, Deezer, Beatport, and more.

Tunecore was the first truly successful music distribution "aggregator" in the market, and I still love their model for a few reasons. As of this writing, Tunecore's fee is $29.99 up front and $49.99/year every subsequent year to distribute an album. Singles cost $9.99/year. Have a think on these numbers. If you are brand new and have no idea what kind of income your release will generate, you should actually distribute via CD Baby, which we'll discuss next. But if you are an artist with a proven sales/streaming track record and know that past individual releases generated more revenue from this distribution channel than $555.44 USD a year, plus Tunecore's annual fee (which varies depending on if your release is an album or single, etc.), go with Tunecore.

CD Baby is the other common option for distribution. They charge, as of this writing, $49 per album or $9.95 per single *plus* 9 percent of your release's distribution income. That is why, if you are a bigger artist, you should go with Tunecore. If just getting going, CD Baby is for you.

If you are a dance artist à la EDM, I encourage you to work with Label Engine. As of this writing, Label Engine charges $7.99 per track and $29.99 per album, with EP and extended album pricing options as well. This will also ensure your music gets onto Beatport, which is essentially the iTunes/download store of dance music.

Beyond that, there is a new platform called Level that offers a variety of free and lower priced distribution options. Truth be told, I have not worked with Level yet, but look forward to checking it out and will post my thoughts on it in the link for updates mentioned in this book's Afterword. There are countless distribution aggregators to work with who have similar terms. ONErpm in particular, also offers video distribution options.

So far, we hope that you've learned to try and find humans at the companies you work with. If this isn't possible with Tunecore and CD Baby, these types of "aggregator" distributors often have options to support you with playlist pitching and download store features. Though, know that CD Baby also hosts conferences for musicians if you want to trek out to meet people from the company. But if not, again, CD Baby offers a variety of free and paid resources to put yourself in the best position to land playlists and features.

Reminder! Please do not check the box to have your publishing collected on by Tunecore or CD Baby, unless you want to. I recommend working with Songtrust, as mentioned, so your publishing collection is in one place instead of spreading out what could be a unified and organized revenue stream for you amongst a variety of companies for no real reason. And double reminder that Songtrust powers CD Baby's publishing collection. So why not go straight to the source?

Distribution Companies

An additional option for distributing your music is via a distribution company such as The Orchard, Redeye, Symphonic, and a myriad of others. These companies are selective in who they work with and charge roughly 15 percent to distribute your music digitally, with some (especially Redeye) also offering physical distribution options, which we'll discuss next. Like any company, it's best if you have a human relationship with your distributor. In theory, it is their job to push for Spotify playlists and Tidal features. To be honest, I'm not sure if that promotion is worth 15 percent, but that is up to you. It's fun when such promotions are landed, but it doesn't necessarily make a long-term impact. That said, every bit of promotion does help the bigger picture, so this is truly up to you.

Many of these companies are the distribution arms for labels, and this can be a way to get in with such companies if your numbers grow high enough. But you certainly shouldn't give up 15 percent on your music distribution thinking that it will get you "signed" to a label. Again, have a think on this, as CD Baby charges a flat fee upon signing up plus 9 percent and will give you the tools or even handle your playlist and download store marketing in some cases. (These cases tend to be with artists who have proven sales and streaming track records from previous releases.) You'll have more competition in landing these features and playlists with an "aggregator," as the people at these companies have many more releases to sort through. That said, I've had countless artists featured on, say, the iTunes store over the years, and on streaming playlists no matter who is pitching them. It doesn't guarantee success. We'll talk about the best methods to get your music onto playlists in the next chapter. But ultimately if you are successful, these playlists will come. Can landing a playlist help your career? For sure! But you will have to decide if you want to pay 6 percent more in distribution fees for something that may or may not happen through a distribution company. (The 6 percent is the difference between CD Baby's 9 percent commission versus the average distributor's cut of 15 percent.)

That all said, I've often gone to distribution companies when an artist needs a little more cash for any reason. Depending on your track record, advance cash payments can happen with distribution companies. But please know that I do this when I've taken on an artist who is in the middle of their album process. Thus, I wasn't involved from day one to dispense all of the advice I've given out in this book so far. Therefore, if an artist needs a little more cash to get to the finish line, I've contacted distributors for an advance in such situations. At the same time, this often gives a company a reason to make your release a priority, but that will be more likely to happen if you create relationships with people at your distribution company. However, when I'm involved from day one, we tend to work with Tunecore or CD Baby, depending on the artist's past distribution revenue history to determine which of the two companies makes the most sense for their career.

Physical Distribution

I'd love to be wrong here, but more often than not, I don't see artists needing physical compact disc distribution if you're just getting going. As you grow, a physical distributor may want to work with you, and that's great! They'll also work with you on digital and vinyl, which means your career has grown large enough that there is demand for CDs. But otherwise, I'd just sell CDs via your website and preorder campaigns, if there is a demand from your fans. Which from indie to dance, I'm still seeing, and CDs are quite reasonably priced to produce. So definitely go for it if this is something your fans are asking for.

Vinyl is another story. No matter what vinyl means to you, be it audio quality or a beautiful merchandise item, it is incredibly relevant. If you included vinyl in your pre-order, and everyone really should, but didn't have a ton of volume in that sales category, you can work with companies such as Diggers' Factory[4] that will let you press vinyl on demand. If your vinyl pre-order numbers are solid, you can work with the companies that we'll list below, which, as of this writing, have minimum order numbers that we'll note. No matter who you go with, be sure to ask if they offer price breaks with certain order quantities. If you are close to hitting that number, it'll save you money in the long run if you order a few more up front that you can sell at shows and on your webstore, which we'll discuss in chapter 9. Also keep in mind where the records are being pressed versus where they will be shipped, as international shipping prices can add up since vinyl is heavy. And plan your timeline accordingly—depending

---

4 https://www.diggersfactory.com/vinyl-on-demand

on how backed up plants are, vinyl can take upward of five months to produce, test, and deliver. At the same time, keep your fans in the loop on the process. The key to customer service is to listen to your fans and keep them engaged and informed throughout the process. The following are vinyl plant options for you to consider, based on your location and how many copies you plan to order:

Minimum of one hundred copies:

- Gotta Groove Records[5]: I've worked with them many times and love them. Note: they require a 50 percent payment up front.

- El Dorado[6]: This company is based in Germany. Note: they require 100 percent payment up-front.

Minimum of three hundred copies:

- United Record Pressing[7]: They've been in the business a long time, and artists tend to love them.

Minimum of five hundred copies:

- Furnace[8] (Virginia)

- Hand Drawn Pressing[9] (Texas)

- SunPress Vinyl[10] (Florida)

---

5 https://www.gottagrooverecords.com/
6 https://www.eldorado-media.com/
7 http://www.urpressing.com/
8 https://www.furnacemfg.com/
9 https://www.handdrawnpressing.com/
10 https://www.sunpressvinyl.com/

- Record Technology Incorporated[11] (RTI) (California)

- Sound Performance[12] (New York City)

- GZ Vinyl[13] (Czech Republic)

Beyond that, if your career is growing to a national level, I encourage you to contact the Coalition of Independent Music Stores[14], or CIMS. The wonderful team at CIMS will solicit your release to independent vinyl shops and place an order to buy your vinyl from you to distribute to these stores on your behalf.

A Note on Pandora and Sign-Up for SoundExchange

As of this writing, all of the above digital distributors also handle Pandora. However, getting music up on Pandora after distributing your music is currently backed up for weeks, so there might be a delay in your music appearing there.

While you're waiting for your music to go live on Pandora, register with SoundExchange. SoundExchange is a nonprofit created by the US government that pays out internet radio royalties to artists and recording rights owners when music is played on internet and satellite radio stations, such as Pandora and SiriusXM. These are "non-interactive" channels where the user can't necessarily choose the specific track they are listening to. For years, SoundExchange even explicitly advertised to and publicly named artists that they had royalties for to track them down and pay them. Don't be one of these artists! Get on it now and register with SoundExchange. You only have to do so once. However, unlike with your PRO (e.g. ASCAP/BMI/SESAC), you must register again if you record under a new name

---

11 http://recordtech.com/
12 https://www.soundperformance.us/
13 http://www.gzvinyl.com/
14 http://www.cimsmusic.com/

or form a new band, group, or project. Double-check your catalog from time to time to ensure everything is in there. SoundExchange pays out monthly or quarterly depending on your revenue level, and we'll discuss those details in chapter 10. And don't worry. We're going to do a revenue stream checklist, also in chapter 10, to ensure you haven't missed a single revenue stream along the way.

Similarly, opt in for Pandora's AMP promotional program, as it can take a few months to get confirmed. AMP offers a suite of tools to check out and promote your latest music and tour dates on Pandora. Once you do have access to Pandora's AMP program, you'll want to record audio messages; CTAs, or calls to action, for your fans; and AMPcasts, which are audio messages recorded on the go.

Indie and Major Labels

This book is assuming that you aren't signed to a label, as the vast majority of musicians in the world are not. If that is a goal, following the steps of this entire book is the best way to get there. So much so that when I'm on panels at conferences with colleagues from major and independent labels, they always agree with that exact statement. In the modern era, a label wants to see that you've done everything in your power to get your career to the highest possible level. Will a label sign someone on pure music/talent alone? Sure, but there are also horror stories of labels signing artists based solely on their recordings, only to realize their live shows aren't yet up to par with the music. Or that the artist doesn't engage with their fans, making the label wonder why they should care and promote the music as well.

If you are on a label, this book is just as important for your long-term career to ensure you engage with fans and are collecting as much data that you own and control (fan email addresses, phone numbers, and location) as possible. This is in case the label changes owners or doesn't exist for as long as you want your career to.

Indubitably, labels distribute music, too, as that was a core function of their initial reason for existing in the first place during the pre-digital era. As mentioned, an independent label will generally receive 50 percent of your master recording revenue after recoupment. Some will own your master recording forever, with others licensing it from you for a set amount of time if the album has recouped. You generally need to give notice within a certain time frame prior to your contract's term ending if you want your master recording rights back.

A major label will roughly receive 85 percent of your master recording revenue after recoupment. Majors will often only work with artists that assign additional rights to them, such as and generally inclusive of merchandising, touring, and/or music publishing. They will almost always own your recordings forever, or in "perpetuity." However, I recently interviewed Freddie Gibbs' manager, Ben "Lambo" Lambert. Lambo and Freddie built Freddie's career over the past decade and they are now able to license Freddie's music to a major; or "rent" it to them as they say. This is a great position to be in, getting one's masters back from a major label after a set amount of time and recoupment, that they worked tremendously hard on their own to obtain.

Personally, I'd rather see artists give a distribution aggregator a small fee and keep the rest of the revenue their music generates, but that choice is up to you. Signing to a label can mean greater success, but that is not guaranteed. If you do have an opportunity to work with a label, I'd recommend signing as short of a commitment as possible and giving it a shot! If it doesn't work out, either for you or because the company closes or sells, and you've followed all of the steps of this book, you'll have a solid fanbase to fall back on. You can then continue to grow that fanbase organically and have an audience for your music forever. Which is ultimately the goal: a sustainable music career for the rest of your life.

CHAPTER 7:

HOW TO MARKET WITH OR WITHOUT A BUDGET

Now it's time to spread the word on your music! Truth be told, this is not always artists' favorite department. Understandably, you want to create art. But everything we will discuss here should come from the heart as well. The best connectors, be it Lady Gaga or Zoë Keating, come from a place of authenticity when communicating with their audiences.

A Note on Attitude

"The grass is always greener on the other side" is a famous phrase for a reason. It's completely understandable to look around and wonder "Why do they have that, and I do not?" I truly believe that if you focus on yourself and your own growth, you'll get there. But if such thoughts continue to arise, reach out to the artists you are looking up to and connect. See if they're willing to have a conversation on how they got to where they are. On one hand, these feelings are potentially more prevalent than ever in the age of social media. On the other, it's that much easier to connect with your peers so you can learn and help each other grow as a community. One of the best ways as a fan to find out about artists is from other artists, be it via retweet or a support slot. Regardless, know that those you admire are most likely looking around at what others have as well, so the best route is to truly focus on yourself and your audience. Pay it forward, and try to help others along the way, as your musician peers might be looking to you for guidance and advice too.

At the same time, know that there isn't a silver bullet for anyone. If there was, all artists would go with this publicist or that agent. It is all about creating great art and connecting with and building your audience. Add some magical positive energy fairy dust on top to get there. Keeping things in perspective with good vibes is only going to help.

Basically, have a positive attitude! There are way worse lives to be living than one that creates art. If you go into situations with a negative outlook, this is going to come back to haunt you. Be mindful of everyone you come into contact with, be it a fan, promoter, industry person, and/or someone doing promotions or work on your behalf. We're human too! If you have concerns about your career and are fortunate enough to work with people supporting you, it's OK to express that in a levelheaded and planned manner. But blaming the city or scene you're a part of or the people spending time and energy helping you out will not only get you nowhere, but you'll also gain a reputation that will make people want to work with other artists and not you.

A Note on Balance

Before we dig in on spreading the word on your music, remember that you are an artist! So try to keep your mind balanced by not losing yourself within marketing and industry work so much so that you're losing sight of your art. As important as everything I'm about to explain is, it's nothing without your creative soul and spirit.

I often advise artists to spend an hour a business day on their social media and emails. (In our case, we use the messaging platform Slack to communicate with many of our artists.) That way you are connecting with your audience, which is crucial. But you aren't getting lost in social media accounts that are literally programmed to be addictive.

The aforementioned Zoë Keating, truthfully the only artist I've ever met that adheres to all of the tenets of this book, takes a different approach. Zoë goes in bursts, spending time directly connecting with her audience. But when it's time to make music, she holes up in the studio and blocks out the rest of the world.

It's up to you! But balance is key, and that can also be found in breaks with friends, a pet, meditation, exercise, or whatever gets you out of your head for a bit.

A Note on Budget

If you have a budget in the range of $1,000 to $1,500, you might want to look into an indie publicist to see if they will service a press release and go after a few press hits for you. We're going to talk about the reality of public relations in the modern music industry later in this chapter, but I wanted to bring this up if you have access to a publicist who feels that they can premiere a new song for you. If so, you're going to have to time your distribution plan so your music is out on major platforms in conjunction with this release. Talk to your publicist to see if they feel that this is a reality, and if it is; great! Work with them to premiere the track using CASH Music's tools via your website if you can code or via Bandcamp's embed codes if you do not know how to code. Some media outlets may ask that you premiere the track using SoundCloud, which is fine, but you won't directly monetize by doing so from stream one. If that's the only way the media outlet premieres music, that's OK, but be ready to go with your music on Bandcamp as soon as the media outlet's premiere window of exclusivity has expired. (Discuss this time period with your publicist; it's generally a day, if that.) And see if the outlet, via your publicist, is up to link to your Bandcamp or pre-order within the press premiere piece regardless, so you don't lose the attention of any fan once they're distracted by something else online.

If you don't have access to, or a budget for, a publicist, truly don't sweat it. I just wanted to get the above out of the way for those who are able to premiere a track, if they so choose. And if you don't have a publicist but do know any local writers or bloggers who dig your music, contact them to see if they'd like to premiere a new track with details on your release. If not, do not fret. It's far from the end of the world if you're just starting out and do not know any music journalists or bloggers yet. Or as you will see, if you don't land any press at all.

Email List, Text Club, and Patreon Announcements

No matter where you are with regard to a track announcement, you'll first want to connect with your loyal email list subscribers. I would send this out as soon as your track premieres and your release is up on Bandcamp. Draft a personal note thanking your subscribers for their support during your creation process. Tell your audience to stay tuned to your preferred social media accounts (which we'll get into, but as of this writing that really should be Facebook, Instagram, and Twitter) for additional announcements of your music's availability on Spotify, Pandora, Tidal, Apple Music, and their favorite music platform. Let them know that the best way to help is to spread the word by sharing your track premiere and/or Bandcamp release on their social media accounts, telling everyone they know about it if they're so inclined, and forwarding this email to friends. If you already have a release show and/or tour dates lined up, include those as well, but it's OK if you don't; I'll teach you how to get that rolling in the following chapter. While you're prepping your mailer, make sure you get an announcement up about all of the above to your Patreon subscribers as well. This is essentially your fan club, so the earlier you can break news to them on everything you're doing, the better. Keep them in mind as you go for anything fun that you want to share with your Patrons along the way that might make more sense for hardcore fans, as opposed to the wider audiences you're developing through your email list and social media accounts. And don't forget about your text club! Message your fans via text to share the news on your release and thank them for their support.

Social Media Announcements

Once you've sent out your mailer, text blast, and informed your Patrons, take the news of your track premiere and/or release to your social media accounts. Be mindful of when you are posting. If you are a night owl who is ready to go at 2:00 a.m. on a weekend, hold off until Monday midday. I like to post on social media during the middle of the day on Mondays and Tuesdays around 1:00 p.m. ET for major announcements, so we are giving equal love to the West Coast, South America, Europe, and Africa. (Sorry, Asia and Australia; I promise that we love you too!) If you are not available to post then, many social media platforms will let you schedule your posts. And for those that don't, there are programs like Hootsuite where you can do just that.

Social Media 101

Typing out posts is not enough! You want to make your posts as engaging as possible to as many people as you can, so the audience not only sees your content but are also encouraged to share your news and music even more widely.

On all social media platforms, tag any and every noun that you can—the media outlet that premiered your track, the journalist who wrote about it, the music platform you're spotlighting (which should be Bandcamp, in my opinion, out of the gate). Get in the habit of this until it's mindless, so you're always tagging venues, promoters, and other artists you're per-forming with. Frankly, most people are terrible at this, so get ahead by showing music platforms, promoters, other artists on the bill, and media outlets that you are putting the effort in. This also tees them up to easily share or retweet what you are saying, spreading the word even further.

On Twitter, as of this writing, it is crucial that if you are opening a post with a tag (e.g., @MilwaukeeRecord rules for premiering my new track!), you must add a period in front of the tag. Otherwise only those following you and the handle you are tagging will see it, severely diminishing the audience for the post. This is because Twitter thinks you're replying to or having a conversation with that account, not doing a post to share with all of your followers. It also shows that you don't really know how to use the platform, which isn't the end of the world, but we want you to get your music out to as many people as possible. Here is the right way to tee up that post: .@MilwaukeeRecord rules for premiering my new track! [link to the track premiere]. Check out the full release here: [link to Bandcamp or your direct to fan platform].

Twitter, and Instagram in particular, are all about #hashtags. You can use up to thirty tags per post on Instagram using 2,200 total characters as of this writing. Choose hashtags that make sense for your post. So if *Milwaukee Record* has premiered your track, and that is also where you are based, throw in hashtags for #Milwaukee, #Wisconsin, and anything else that you think makes sense. You can do this on Facebook too, though hashtags tend to be most effective on Instagram and Twitter.

Until you you are filling massive venues, I encourage you to reply to all sane tweets, favorite all Instagram comments that you dig, like appropriate Facebook posts, and reply to all Facebook, Instagram, and Twitter direct messages that make sense. This can get overwhelming, and that's where I suggest setting limits for yourself of, say, an hour a day. If you're getting quite a few emails about your music, include this in your hour as well, so you don't fry your brain and lose sight of being an artist. And when you are selling out large venues, still engage, but know that you're human and getting back to everyone isn't realistic, or necessarily healthy for one's well being in my experience.

If you feel like you have all of the above mastered, try experimenting with Facebook and Instagram Live, as well as Instagram and Facebook "Stories," which can be anything from a still image to a video to a previously recorded live stream. You can add "extras" like the date, temperature, and different fonts or not. Similarly, as mentioned, if Snapchat and TikTok appeal to you, integrate these platforms into your strategy. Take it all one step at a time, and whenever you get overwhelmed, take a break.

Also play around with YouTube. Artists like Julia Nunes (whom, full disclosure, I manage) have embraced the platform and grown a loyal following. Metadata tags are crucial here. So make sure you add as many tags as the platform allows. This can include your artist name, the style of music, your hometown, and anything else that you can think of that might boost your video in the platform's algorithms to pair you with like-minded fans. What also supports YouTube's current algorithms is posting regularly; so keep this in mind as well.

Engagement and Growth

Growing your career is your job at any level, no matter the promotional team you have on hand. Continue to post on your social media at least a few times a week, following all of the above guidelines, and your base really will continue to grow. Invite friends to like your artist page on Facebook. If Twitter intimidates you, view it as a river of information. This was the strategy a colleague of mine suggested to Lenny Kravitz and John Legend when helping them set up their Twitter accounts over a decade ago when the concept was new. What do you like? Say, a sports team, a news outlet, and other artists. Start following accounts you are into and jump into the river of information and conversation when you're ready.

The Golden Rule of Social Media

I have one simple rule for social media posting that has never steered me wrong. I try to only post positive statements on the internet. Frankly,

I joined Twitter sarcastically in 2008, thinking to myself, "Maybe someone will care about a young woman starting an entertainment company." Shortly after, *Billboard* named me a must-follow executive on Twitter multiple years in a row. The rare times I do gripe about something on social media, it has always come back to bite me. So keep it positive, and you really can't go wrong.

Email List Growth via Noisetrade

Another way to grow your email list with a new release is by reaching out to the great team at Noisetrade to see if they'll give away your new song for email addresses, along with promotion and editorial. As of this writing, Noisetrade has over one million fan users who utilize this platform to trade their data for new music. Data that you can then own and control moving forward.

Pinned Posts, Ads, and Followers

Pin your track/Bandcamp announcement on your Facebook and Twitter page, and be mindful of when you want to swap that out for a tour or other announcement. But also be on top of swapping that back out for your music once the tour wraps so the posts are current. Same goes for your social media accounts' URL / weblink in your bio.

If you have even a few dollars a day to spend on Facebook or Instagram ads, I encourage you to do so to boost your release announcement and increase your page likes. Facebook is a company built on advertising revenue, so this really does work. Keep that in mind for live and tour date posts as well. If you don't have any money to spend on Facebook ads, that's OK too. I don't think Twitter ads are as necessary, as you can grow your audience using the organic methods we've outlined above. Same with Instagram, but since they are owned by Facebook, ad strategies can be effective there. But if you don't have a budget for Instagram ads, utilize all of the above tips to grow your audience naturally.

We'll talk more about this in chapter 12, but having followers on any social media outlet does not mean those in the industry will care. What we're looking for is great art, and regular engagement on your social media. If we see large numbers and your music isn't great, we'll assume you are using technology or money to gain followers and will see right through it. If your music is awesome but you haven't posted on your social media in a year, why should we care about spreading the word more than you do? If working with major industry people and organizations is a goal, create great art and follow everything in this chapter to grow your career. As that is exactly what industry professionals are looking for.

Music Platform Announcements, Plus a Spotify and Pandora Deep Dive

As your fans are alerted that your music is live on Spotify, Pandora, and other major music platforms, tell your followers on social media! This gives you an excuse to continue to post about your music's release, albeit with a slightly different message via a new platform announcement. Also, tag these outlets so they know that you are spreading the word about your music as well.

I'm hearing less of this as of late, but if you still feel overwhelmed by social media, definitely check out my friend Ariel Hyatt's books. She has put together tremendous resources that go into further detail on social media specifically for musicians, whereas I've just covered the basics for you to grow your career.

Additionally, Ariel has written excellent guides for getting verified, growing your following, and getting on Spotify playlists, in addition to the resources that your distributor has provided you with. Instead of lifting her material for this book, I urge you to head over to Ariel's "Indie Musicians Guide To Spotify: Part 1 Build Your Foundation[15]," (available

---

15 https://cyberprmusic.com/indie-musicians-guide-spotify-part-one/

for free online), with part 3 specifically covering "How To Get On Spotify Playlists[16]." Follow Ariel on Twitter via @CyberPR[17] to stay in the loop on all of the great details and advice she regularly dispenses.

SoundCloud

Use your best judgement regarding SoundCloud. As of this writing, SoundCloud does not monetize your music from stream one. Our company primarily uses SoundCloud to host unreleased music privately to share internally with industry colleagues. Obviously for many genres—not at all limited to hip-hop, EDM, and more—it is an incredible platform for discovery. So if you feel that your audience is using SoundCloud, definitely upload your music there. Add a link to your Bandcamp or direct to fan release platform, email list link, and text club signup on your Soundcloud page to try and not miss a single fan for future communications on your work. I generally want artists' music any and everywhere. But if you don't feel like you'll get much out of the scene at SoundCloud, I'm OK with you skipping it to ideally point your audience to your website or Bandcamp from the get go. As the aforementioned platforms are where you will receive the highest profit margins. Or even Spotify, which is the number one traditional music streaming platform and is generally easy for fans to access and listen to. At least you're getting *something* per stream with Spotify, as opposed to nothing and no fan retention on SoundCloud.

Marketing with Any Level of Budget

If you have some funds to promote your music, good for you! Now let's use them wisely, as otherwise you're throwing your money down the drain.

Press/Public Relations (PR)

Most artists tend to gravitate toward wanting a publicist for their first promotional, or promo, step. I have mixed

---

16 http://bit.ly/SpotifyPlaylistsCyberPR
17 https://twitter.com/cyberpr

feelings about this. Not because there isn't value in having someone work you to press. It is more that we need to be clear on what the goals are so that everyone is on the same page.

In the pre-digital era, when I happened to be a teenager and voracious music fan, we would read about music in a physical magazine, decide that sounded like something we wanted to check out, get in our cars, drive to a record store, and (in my era) buy a physical CD. Then we'd drive home to listen to it or listen right away in our cars if we were lucky enough to have a vehicle with a CD player. That is a lot of steps! But notice what I said first: we read about music in a physical magazine. Radio was a factor as well, which we'll talk about next, but a placement in *Spin* magazine in the 90s had a clear "return on investment," or ROI.

Unfortunately for my publicist friends, currently this ROI is far less direct. That doesn't mean we don't love publicists or PR campaigns! But I am very up front with artists who hire publicists. My goal is to score a solid link or two, or a few, on your music from reputable media outlets. We can then send these links to your synch pitching companies, agents who represent tours we are pitching you for support slots on, and really to anyone we're trying to get to pay attention to your music. It shouldn't matter, but being written about does help to at least get those we're pitching on your behalf to hopefully click on your music and listen. Which is just a first step, but hopefully it helps to get you in the door and additionally helps to reinforce the great organic work you are already doing on your own.

That said, even if you get a publicist who lands you in Stereogum or Brooklyn Vegan and that's what you think will solely take you to the next level, that is rarely the case. I've had countless artists score placements in such outlets, and if there isn't organic momentum otherwise, it's hard for a single piece of press to change your career. Of course there are stories—Bon Iver comes to mind—of an artist landing a Pitchfork piece and having their career explode[18]. Frankly, that's akin to winning the lottery. I've had many artists on Pitchfork. Definitely push any piece of press you land out everywhere and use it to open more doors. But, generally speaking, careers don't necessarily drastically change as soon as a Pitchfork review, or any single piece of press is landed. Consider press hits to be a tool to utilize in your career, not the end goal.

PR Budgets

With all of this in mind, I encourage you to be mindful of what you spend on PR. Your publicist is going to get paid no matter what; paying a high monthly fee does not guarantee success. Meet with the publicist you are interested in to discuss what they feel are realistic goals based on the stage of career you are at. If you are just getting going, I recommend that you see if someone is willing to do a press release and try to land a few pieces by following up for $1,000 to $1,500. We will discuss tour press in the next chapter. Many publicists will quote you higher. Many publicists will be mad at me for listing these types of prices in this book. The goal is for you all to grow together, not to

---

18 I recently had the absolute privilege of interviewing Justin Vernon of Bon Iver, who clarified that My Old Kentucky Blog is the outlet that initially posted his songs from Myspace in which his career subsequently rapidly changed, but you get the idea. Note that he also added that this happened without a publicist, or anyone, pitching his music to My Old Kentucky Blog.

blow your wad on two months of a publicist so you have nothing left to live off of.

<u>Help Your Publicist Help You: Asset Organization and Respectful Communication</u>

Before you begin with a publicist, they are going to expect that you have press photos ready to go, that you own the rights to or have permission to use, with credit. Don't overthink this. You are a creative person who most likely has access to a smartphone, which contains a nicer camera than what anyone other than the highest level of photographers had access to in the pre-digital era. Get some press shots together, and be ready to deliver high-resolution versions to your publicist, noting the photographer's credit, so you are ready to go on day one.

Also, have links handy to your music on Spotify for your publicist, as well as high-quality MP3 files in case they want those as well. Send them a list of your organized social media links, and ask if there is anything else that you can do to make their job more seamless.

My company has a rule of responding to all emails within twenty-four business hours. That means if we get a message at, say, 4:00 p.m. on a Friday, I'll respond to it by 4:00 p.m. on Monday. I mentioned this to a publicist friend over lunch one day, and she literally almost fell out of her chair. She was blown away by the concept. As when she sends out press releases, artists are understandably excited, but blow up her inbox, emailing her multiple times a day to ask if she has received responses. All you are doing by emailing a publicist, or any industry person, multiple times a day is making it harder for them to do their job and get back to you with the information that you want. So be mindful about when you are checking in, and think about doing so later in the week. And, if you set up Google Alerts, you'll get the information you're looking for anyway. You can also google yourself and click on the "news" tab to see what has popped up in the meantime, freeing your publicist up to proactively continue to work on your behalf. My publicist friend has since put the twenty-four business hour rule into her email signature for everyone's benefit—hers and musicians alike.

With regard to the other end of the enthusiasm scale—make yourself available for your publicist or anyone working on your promotional team, as well as for the writers they are targeting on your behalf. The following tweet from a music journalist and editor caught my eye and sums this up well:

Stephen Carlick
@stephencarlick

Follow

Publicist: Please interview this band
Publicist: Please interview this band
Publicist: Please interview this band
Publicist: Please interview this band
Publicist: Please interview this band
Me: Okay sure
Publicist: Oh cool yeah k lemme see if
they're doing interviews

10:14 PM - 22 Jan 2019

331 Retweets 4,404 Likes

71   331   4.4K

When I read this, the artist comes off as being too busy to prioritize something the publicist has landed. Don't be this artist! Help your publicist, and anyone doing promotion on your behalf, to help you by being available. This will allow anyone working on your behalf to spend the majority of their time working on securing opportunities, instead of chasing you and following up to seize on what they have landed.

Sustainable PR

Traditional publicists might hate what I'm about to say next, but it really can help them as well. Every time you land any sort of press, be it on your own, organically, or via a publicist, grab that journalist's email address and Twitter handle, and pop it into a Google spreadsheet. Our office calls ours a "Fancy Friends" list for each artist. This is a great way to keep track of tastemaker types who support your music. By growing this list, you have a way to communicate directly with people who are already into what you're doing. Just like that, you can keep them in the loop about tour dates—always offering to put them on the guest list—in addition to music videos, remixes, and other news you might not have the budget for a publicist to handle. This way you can then still share what you're up to in hopes that they help spread the word on it. Set up Google Alerts for yourself so you do not miss a single mention of your work in the media, and also file away the press report you're given at the end of a PR campaign to reference in the future. If you're not given a press report from a publicist after a campaign, ask for one.

Compiling these contacts also ensures that when you do have a budget for a publicist, they and you aren't starting from scratch every time. Is it frustrating when you work with a publicist and they've only landed press based on your contacts? Yes, but just know that you are doing something right on your own, and maybe PR doesn't always make sense. And, make sure your publicist knows you have those relationships already, making it clear that you're hiring them to hopefully expose your music to additional journalists.

Radio

American radio is a beast, no doubt. If you feel that you have a shot at what is known as Adult Album Alternative, or AAA radio, track down someone with ears like my friend who works promotions for the AAA format that was mentioned in chapter 1. If you're onto something, they'll take you on, for a relatively reasonable fee. Otherwise, go to local radio events hosted by stations in your genre to get to know people who work there. Send organized emails with *links* to download your music—*never* send attachments, which clog up inboxes—to a dedicated local music show host. Do not blanket email and spam as many radio contacts as you can find.

Realistically, to get played on pop or country radio, you'll need to be on a major label or have an equally major budget.

Otherwise, you can try and send your music to NPR, if critical darling independent music is your thing. The NPR Music team is on Twitter, as are many curators and DJs, so seek people like this out. Offer to get them on the guest list for your shows, and be mindful that you're not overcommunicating, as you don't want to spam them.

College Radio

College radio, unfortunately, meant a lot more with regard to career results in the pre-digital era. To such a degree that a college radio campaign is now often relatively reasonably priced, as low as $500, but sometimes more. Companies like Powderfinger, Terrorbird, Planetary Group, and The Syndicate are great places to start.

But similar to PR, know that your return on investment will be indirect. You will hopefully score interviews, in-studio performances, and maybe even land yourself on the college radio charts. However, use all of these opportunities and links as items to share with your audience on social media, as well as with your email list and Patreon subscribers. Use any college radio chart placements as a talking point for your synch company and when pitching for support (opening) tours, which we'll talk more about in the following chapter. Otherwise, know that if you don't utilize the strategies in this paragraph, most college radio stations, despite also being internet stations, don't have much literal bandwidth or audience reach. However, your fans don't know that, so spread the word that you're getting played on college stations, as that will hype up your audience to keep listening and sharing your music from there. At the same time, there are college stations with large followings such as KCRW in Los Angeles, WFUV in New York, KUTX in Austin, and WERS in Boston. Start to pay attention to where you are getting spins, as these larger stations can positively impact your career and lead to airplay on commercial stations and new fans.

Additionally, you can gain indirect growth from college campaigns solely due to the fact that college radio music directors tend to be the tastemaker types among their group and circles of friends. Although it's not guaranteed, this is a great way to get your music in front of these students as they grow their careers, as some go on to work in music professionally. Or simply so they share that they love your music on their social media to their friends and networks, who often know them as their "music friend" that exposes them to new artists they might like.

Always let your radio promo team know that you're available for interviews and in-studio performances. Offer them, as well as all college radio teams, guest list spots for your shows and tickets for them to give away on air, which also inherently promotes your show.

<u>Specialty Radio</u>
There are also "specialty" radio campaigns that cost more than college radio campaigns but way less than commercial radio campaigns. This will get you on shows specific to your genre, and most of my experience here has been in indie/alternative radio. I've had artists make it onto specialty radio charts, and that's great. We use it as a talking point similar to what I describe above with college radio charting, but it doesn't necessarily move the needle on careers much otherwise.

Regardless, as always, connect with music directors and DJs on social media, engage, retain their information, and continue to respectfully keep them in the loop on the latest and greatest talking points on your career (press, shows, etc.) And again, offer them guest list spots to shows and tickets to give away to their audiences.

<u>Podcasting</u>
Another way to grow your audience is to launch a podcast. An artist we manage, Fox Stevenson, has done just that, as he wanted to make a deeper connection with his audience than the engagement he already does on social media. I think this is brilliant, and if it appeals to you, I encourage you to do the same. You already know how to record, and there are a variety of distributors out there, with new ones arising every day, to get your podcast out on all major platforms.

Music Videos

Music videos are another medium where the return on investment used to be immense if you scored rotation on MTV or VH1. Videos are obviously still very relevant in a variety of ways (from meme to long-form films), but now you're competing with way more videos and content. Not to mention YouTube technically being the number one platform for streaming music on the planet.

At the same time, you now have access to video equipment like never before. This Young Hines' video[19] was shot on a smartphone! Truly amazing. If this sounds intimidating to you, ask around, and see if any local film students might be interested in collaborating to build their reel and grow together.

If you have a budget for music videos, sorry, filmmaker friends, I don't think you should break the bank here, unless this is deeply important to your creative vision and you have a ton of cash lying around. Again, you want to be smart about what and where you're spending. So use the many tools at your disposal to shoot and edit music videos, and don't feel like you need to make an epic production out of the gate. And see if you can shoot more than one music video at once to maximize budgets, equipment, and time.

Also! If you do make music videos, utilize your publicist and fancy friends list to arrange a video premiere or to get journalists and bloggers to hopefully write about your new clip(s).

Brand, Sponsor, and Endorsement Partnerships

Brand, sponsor, and endorsement partnerships can happen on local, national, and international levels. They are discussed regularly at music conferences, so I do want to bring them up. As with any sort of partnership,

---

19 https://youtu.be/xZAzjHneul8

you want these relationships to be authentic. I consider partnerships to be truly that—a situation where both parties benefit.

However, such partnerships are never guaranteed at any level, which is why I don't particularly love that they are brought up so often. They work for some artists but frankly, very few and definitely not all artists.

That said, get both creative and realistic here. Are there any local brands that might want to partner with you for mutually beneficial promotion? The realistic component is that this is mutually beneficial after you've built a following. So one step at a time. Also keep in mind if a sponsor for your podcast makes sense.

And no matter how much you love the brand, make sure what you sign up for is respectful and makes sense for your audience. I recently had an artist partner with a major music gear company, one that I've worked with many times before. Unfortunately, the ad agency that the brand hired this time around had clearly never worked with artists. They were constantly editing, and frankly cheesing up, an otherwise authentic message from an artist who has built a great audience by being herself otherwise. So know that these partnerships can generate revenue, but don't agree to spamming your followers. That is a losing proposition for both the brand and you.

But now it's time to get your live act together! This is a great way to connect with audiences locally, on the web, and internationally. So get ready to start playing out.

CHAPTER 8:

YOUR LIVE STRATEGY AND EFFICIENT TOURING

N ow it's time to bring your music to life with live shows! Which may or may not include hitting the road initially. In this chapter, we're going to discuss a slew of strategies on how to build your live career, instead of just trekking out to the unknown and hoping for the best.

Practice Makes Perfect

This should kind of go without saying, but there are plenty of instances of artists creating incredible recordings and then suddenly being lost when it's time to hit the stage. Similar to getting your art together for recording, as discussed in chapter 1, you will need to do the same for your live show. Again, most artists know this, so get your set tight and ready to go before you start playing out. If you have grown quickly, maybe see if you can score some bar or open mic gigs, even under a pseudonym, instead of starting with a large hometown or high-profile show. I bring this up as I know of an artist that was signed to a major label and debuted at SXSW. I'm surprised that the label had not seen the artist perform prior to this. But ultimately as soon as they did play a show, the label realized the act did not have the live experience to premiere at a high-profile event. So practice until your live show is ready for others to see, hear, and experience. If you're feeling overwhelmed as you bring studio sounds into the live space, check out Mark Eckert's ebook, *Performing Live*[20].

Hometown Love/Booking a Show 101

Most artists will have some sort of a draw in the place they call home. Reach out to a venue that you feel you can *realistically* draw at least half of the venue's capacity. I say realistically because it's really hard to get people off the couch and out the door to pay for an event and stand for hours. I constantly tell everyone in my life, even if they're planning a party, to not expect everyone who said they'll definitely be there to show up. That said, for your music release show, you're going to want to put every ounce of effort possible into getting friends, family, and fans to turn out.

Let the promoter/talent buyer/venue know that this will be your music release show and that you'd like to put a bill together for it. Depending on the size of the venue, the promoter may come back to you and let you know that you're the second or so "hold" for this date. If you are ready to go for your target date or dates, let them know that you would like to "challenge" for this date. Then, the promoter will go to the agent or artist who has the "first hold" for the date and give them a deadline to confirm or pass, and otherwise the date is yours.

The buyer will then make you some sort of offer. At the local level for a hometown show, go for a door deal. This means you'll receive 80 to 90 percent of the ticket sales, and it's up to you if you want to pay your support acts a flat rate or go all-in together and each share a percentage of ticket sales. If you are headlining and going the latter route, I'd ask for at least half of the take. If you've booked opening acts that legitimately draw, share the remainder with them accordingly, say 25 percent and 25 percent. Use your best judgement here based on each artist's size and ability to get people out to the show. I would keep your ticket price low

---

20 https://www.mark-eckert.com/ebook/

for this show, as it's going to help you out in the long run if you can draw a solid amount of people in your home market while you grow your career. You can also get a "guarantee," which is a set fee you'll be paid, plus generally 85 percent after the promoter has recouped all expenses for the show. But again, this is most likely going to be your strongest market, so I say go for a door deal to maximize your profit margin if you know that people will come out for your show.

How to Promote your Show(s)

You're going to want to really focus in on this date. Most venues have what is called a "radius clause," where you cannot play their city or market a few weeks before or a few weeks after the date. This is good for you as well, as you want to put all of your energy and attention into your release show instead of spreading your audience out among a variety of local dates.

Email, Text List & Social Media Announcements

Once the show and bill are confirmed, ask the promoter when you are OK to announce. They will provide this information to you along with a ticket link or on-sale date. Start working on a mailer to your email list to announce the show and plan to schedule your social media posts so the show information goes live as soon as you have the green light to announce. Do the same with your fan text list. *Do not* announce until you have permission to. It is not the end of the world to leak a live show announcement at the local level. But get in the habit of coordinating with the promoter, as you can, say, get kicked off a Coachella bill for leaking a show before the date it is to be announced. So let's get it right from day one.

Social Media Promotion

Make sure you tag the venue, promoter, and other artists on the bill so they can easily share and retweet your posts. This will also show the promoter that you're putting the work in to get as many people out as possible—which will encourage them to book you again and maybe even support national acts when they come through town. Also ask the promoter if they are doing a Facebook Event for the show or if they'd like for you to initiate one. If they're taking lead, ask them to make you a co-host, so you can invite everyone you know who might be interested in attending.

PR + Social Media

Ask the promoter if they have a press list they'd be up to share and, if not, if you can provide a press release for them to service. You want this press release to be a one page PDF[21], with organized formatting and links to your latest and greatest highlights, your new release, and the show you are promoting. Send your press release out on the closest non-holiday Monday or Tuesday that you can once you have the green light to announce your show. Wednesdays are OK, but do not send a press release out Thursday through Sunday. The goal is for your press release to get read! Also, don't forget a subject line for the email that you send out to journalists with the attached press release. The following Monday or Tuesday, reach out to individual journalists with streaming links, (not downloads), to your new music and offer them guest list spots to your release show. If you have any national press or news in so far, share that with them as well, to further entice journalists and bloggers to check out your work.

---

21 You can create your press release in Google Drive or most word processing programs such as Microsoft Word. Download the document into the PDF format under File, Download and select PDF, for example, in Google Drive.

Retweet any posts from fans who express excitement for the show. Share any press hits or show announcements you get in the media, tagging the publication and journalist accordingly. Follow all of these accounts as well.

Entice Your Fans To Push Your Show For You

If or when there is a lull in excitement, launch a post with the ticket link, letting your audience know that anyone who retweets the link will be entered in a drawing to be on the guest list, and the winner will be announced and contacted the day before the show. This way you're inherently encouraging your audience to promote the show and giving them a chance for you to reward them for doing so. Do the same contest with fans who share your Facebook Event and comment on a similar Instagram post; always tagging the venue, promoter, and other artists on the bill so they continue to spread the word as well.

Ground Game

You can also launch a street team, especially if you live in a market where posting physical posters and flyering is effective. Put up a social media post asking for volunteers, and arm those fans with physical posters and postcards, (that you pay for), in exchange for guest list entry to the show. Have your street team members send you photos to confirm their work around town.

Merchandise Prep

We'll talk about merchandise more in the next chapter. But get your merch plan together for this show, as this should be a strong revenue stream for you in your hometown. If your vinyl isn't ready yet, let fans order it at the gig and tell them when it's estimated to arrive. Since this is your hometown show, see if there is a friend or a family member who might be up to handle the merch table for you. Arm them with your email list and text club sign up details. And if you don't have a large budget for mech, order some stickers and buttons/badges to sell and create any homemade items that you can. You can often sell creative and home-made merchandise at a higher price point, as such items are truly unique and special. Order a Square reader in advance so you can accept credit and debit card sales. Accepting credit and debit cards can often double an artist's merchandise sales, so consider it a piece of gear, and make sure it is on hand at every show. Not to mention that you also collect fans' email addresses with credit card devices such as Square. If possible, have your merchandise person ask fans if you can add their email address to your email list. Otherwise you can send them a BCC'd email at a later time asking permission to add them to your email list. Maybe create a business email address just for such uses, to keep your personal email address private.

Finally, always head out to meet fans for selfies and signing merchandise, etc. after your set. This is an incredible way to not only increase your merch sales but also to make a human connection with fans that can last forever. When I began managing Julia Nunes, I went to cover our mer-chandise table for our intern during the last few songs, so the intern could watch the show. I was surprised when the moment the show ended, Julia sprinted to the merchandise table, out of breath. Most musicians I know tend to take a sip of water or a break before heading to the merch table. Not Julia. Maybe this is why her merch line extended the length of a New York City block (I'm not kidding). I told her I'd rarely, if ever, seen a fan line for merchandise that long. She said she has heard that countless times over the years at her shows. Be like Julia in this instance to make genuine connections with your audience that last a lifetime.

Regional Touring

Congrats on your successful hometown release show! Now it's time to le-verage this into regional dates. I do not think you should blindly tour oth-erwise. Drumming legend and music business guru Martin Atkins points out in his incredible book, *Tour Smart*, that the vast majority of the largest touring markets in the United States are east of the Mississippi River. Therefore if you happen to live east of the Mississippi, and statistically speaking you most likely do, hold off on booking a West Coast tour until it makes sense. And I'll explain exactly when that time is in this chapter.

First, you want to build up your audience regionally. Say you were able to get one hundred fans out for your album release show. Awesome! Reach out and find artists that you are into in the two or three markets that are closest to you. If you are in Milwaukee—I grew up there, which is why I keep referencing it—find artists in Chicago, Madison, Minneapolis, and Iowa City. Let them know you'd like to offer them an opening slot for you in your hometown and want to see if you could set up a "gig swap" to do the same. This is a *great* way to organically build your audience, while (dare I say it) building your network among your fellow musicians. Besides the fact that building a community is fun, it can also help your career. (We'll talk later in this chapter about how.) The internet is such an incredible resource to contact other musicians. It was obviously much harder to do so in the pre-digital era. It surely still happened, but not in a manner as fluid, quick, or seamless as it does today.

No matter where you're touring, follow the same steps you took to promote the show(s) that you did for your release show. Especially with regard to using social media and viral promotion. But also by asking if the venue is willing to share a press list, and if not, if they will service a press release that you draft for them. And, as always, if you have any team members working with you for synch, PR, or radio, let them know your tour dates as soon as they exist so they can spread the word. Always let them know that they have access to guest list spots as needed.

Let Metrics Guide the Way

Whether you are just getting going, or have an established career, pay close attention to your audience's metrics on social media, streaming platforms, and from your website. If you're using Squarespace for your website, it has analytics built in, and really, any modern web platform does at this point. But if it doesn't, add Google Analytics to your website immediately.

Facebook "Insights," which is what Facebook calls metrics on artist pages, is incredibly helpful for tour strategies—no matter the size of your career. If you are based in the Midwest, but realize you have a slew of fans in Austin, it's time to start contacting artists in Texas to gig swap with. See if you can tour your way there and back, ideally supporting other artists along the way. *No matter* the size of the audience you're playing to, play your heart out. Get those five email addresses for your list. And know that you're getting better every day as a musician when you do so. When I was an intern at VH1, I was lucky enough to help out on a shoot one day when my boss was interviewing Michael Stipe of R.E.M. This was in the early 2000s, when The Strokes were first on the scene and taking off. Michael was asked what he thought of such a phenomenon, and he said it was something he didn't envy. He stated that one thing that made R.E.M. what it became was the fact that that they were allowed to develop for years live and play to small or no audiences in bars. That is truly what made them come together as a live band and unit, and the rest is music history. And you never know who will be in the audience! This is more for events like SXSW, but I've had artists play to ten people and land a European booking agent. Or I once heard a story about a low-attended showcase where the band saw someone kind of oddly dancing at the back of the room. As that person got closer, they realized it was Thom Yorke of Radiohead rocking out. Radiohead's long-time producer, Nigel Godrich, ended up producing the band's next album. Whether a music legend is in the audience or not, perform from your soul to gain every fan you can and win over the venue/promoter so they book you again as you grow.

International Touring

This really is more of a subheading for metrics, but obviously it's a larger level than domestic touring and deserves its own category. Start to pay attention to what your metrics are telling you your strongest countries are—you might surprise yourself. I managed an artist who would regularly sell out shows in his home base of Nashville, as well as in London. Yet I noticed that Sao Paulo and Brazil were his number one city and country on Facebook Insights by far. I asked the artist's agent to see what she could drum up for Brazil, and lo and behold, a slew of offers came in.

Similarly, Imogen Heap happened to notice that Jakarta was her number one country on Facebook. Odd, since it's obviously a city, and was outperforming entire countries. Imogen and her manager asked if the agent could reach out to Indonesia to see what she could find. The agent said there was no point because there was no music industry there. They asked again if she could please try, and the agent was surprised to come back with a slew of extremely strong live date offers. The pre-digital music industry focused on North America, Europe, Asia, and maybe Australia and South America if the artist wasn't too burned out by the time they made it through the first three continents. Now there is no limit to connecting with fans, whether there is a traditional music industry where they live or not. Also ask any international promoter or venue you are working with if there are specific visa requirements for you when entering their country to perform.

House Shows

House shows and tours are great new revenue streams and unforgettable experiences for fans that have become more commonplace in the modern era. This is because, with the evolution of the internet, it's now possible to connect artists with hosts in a much more organized manner, as well as to collect payments digitally.

You obviously want to be smart and safe about doing so. We recommend working with reputable companies such as Undertow[22], an organization that works with hosts who regularly open their homes for artists to perform at with fans. Concerts in Your Home[23] is another reputable company to work with and has even expanded to producing a festival. Side Door[24] is a new company that also supplies alternative venues and access to hosts. Some of these companies rely on ratings systems for hosts, ala Airbnb. Please never play a house show alone for additional safety precautions.

It's also on you to professionalize the situation. I have the honor of managing Julia Nunes, who has built an incredible career connecting with her audience and has played countless house shows as national tours. Here is her process, sent out to hosts in advance, to put all involved at ease:

- Clear a space for people to sit. (Usually that means chairs and couches against the wall.)

- Set two chairs and two waters at the front space where all the seating is facing. (Totally OK for there to be no seating.)

- People arrive at 7:00 p.m. at the earliest.

- Julia arrives at 7:45 p.m., sets up her merch table, plays at 8:00 p.m. sharp.

- Show ends at 9:15 p.m.

- Julia sells merch until 10:30 p.m. at the latest.

---

22 https://undertowshows.com/
23 https://concertsinyourhome.org/
24 https://sidedooraccess.com/

- By then there's only a few people left. Julia takes some time to make sure the hosts get any merchandise they want and a free Polaroid, and then they go!

This way, the hosts have a clear plan, and Julia and her co-musician, Chase, book lodging separately for everyone's safety and privacy.

Note that I have also had artists utilize house shows when they are supporting larger artists at traditional venues. Although support tour slots are coveted, they can pay anywhere from $100-$250 a show, or higher depending on your draw. But such numbers aren't always sustainable financially. Thus, alternative venue shows are a great way to increase your tour income on off nights.

Webcasts

If you are starting out or unable to tour for any reason, get rolling with webcasts! This is a great way to connect with your audience and generate income via digital ticket sales, no matter where you are in the world. The aforementioned Julia Nunes has done just that using StageIt,[25] with others using YouNow for webcasting in a variety of forms. You can also offer merchandise discounts via your web store, which we'll discuss in chapter 9, so you have a merch "table" available to generate revenue that way as well. And many webcast platforms offer options for fans to "tip" you beyond the digital ticket they already purchased for the show. We'll keep you posted via a link in this book's Afterword as new platforms that we recommend arise. Regardless of whether you can tour or not, strategically launch live shows via webcast either way! Maybe something special for a certain holiday or event. Get creative here to engage with your fans and grow your audience.

---

25 https://www.stageit.com

What Agents Are Looking For

Almost every artist I've ever met wants a booking agent more than any other team member. To be honest, having one is almost pointless unless you are following all of the above in this chapter and book. Most agents will agree with me on that! If they're just booking you randomly without any information or marketing muscle behind the dates, what's the point? And even if you draw some fans with that method, it maximizes everyone's time and energy to do so properly, to bring in the largest possible audience that you can.

Regardless, let's talk about what agents do want to see when taking on an artist. Generally speaking, agents are very number- and spreadsheet-oriented people. I booked a tour once many years ago, and I was terrible at it! Management takes a great deal of organization as well, but it's a creative, bigger picture and requires a different mind-set than routing and booking tours do. What agents want to know is what your draw is in a variety of markets. They're not necessarily going to care about just your home market, as drawing well there should be a given. They want to know if the word on your music is spreading regionally, nationally, and even internationally. Will an agent take you on if they absolutely love your music and there isn't much of a draw yet? Sometimes, but this is rare and feels like it is becoming rarer every day. I know beloved national acts that have been dropped by their agencies for not drawing enough fans to their shows. So know that as of this writing, a lot of agencies are focusing on the number of tickets you can sell above and beyond all - great art included.

How to Land Support Tours

I feel that one reason many artists may also want an agent is that they think this is their ticket to opening for larger artists. This isn't necessarily the case. Artists want to tour with people they like, their friends, and the music they're into. Remember when I mentioned building a community with fellow artists? You'll only be successful doing so if these relationships are genuine, but this is exactly how to get on bills and open for larger acts as well. Artists make these decisions. Sure, they can be influenced by agents, managers, and others. But at the end of the day, artists want to tour with music and people they like. The Dresden Dolls scored an opening slot for Nine Inch Nails when Trent Reznor saw one of their DIY videos on MTV2 late one night. That wouldn't have happened without Trent, no matter who The Dresden Dolls were working with, myself included.

Maximizing Tour Profits

One way to really make money as you grow is to be mindful of tour costs and expenses. If you've grown to a national touring level based on your music and live set; that's awesome! I completely understand the value of production; I was a global tour manager for many years early in my career. However, if you've gotten to where you are and are getting bigger and have, say, a tour manager, sound person, lighting person, merchandise person, and monitor/stage tech, do you need an instrument tech for everyone on stage? Would your crew be up to share rooms to increase their pay a bit, which is way less than what individual rooms would cost? Do you really need a tour bus?

I was in Australia once on tour, and Ben Folds stopped by a show for the artist I was tour managing. He told us about how his business manager presented him with two tour budgets one day - one with and without a tour bus. When he realized he'd do exponentially better financially by forgoing a bus, he said he had no problem rolling up to late night TV shows in a van.

Keep all of this in mind as you grow. Touring is hard, but there are way worse jobs in the world. And it is a job. Although it is nice to have a full crew and a tour bus that costs thousands of dollars *a day*, see if you can keep the crew that got you to where you are. Do this before you go nuts expanding your tour expenses to spend on every bell and whistle available.

VIP Packages

As you grow, keep VIP packages and fan experiences in mind for an additional revenue stream. This could be access to soundcheck, an exclusive merchandise item, or whatever you feel will enhance the live experience for your fans. I've worked with the Zac Brown Band, in which Zac is an incredible cook, and does "Eat & Greets" with his fans. He now has his own line of barbeque sauces. Think about what you would enjoy as a fan, as well as authentic and genuine experiences that you are comfortable delivering. The opportunities are infinite here.

Recording Your Shows

One element of the modern music industry that I'm surprised hasn't taken off more is getting creative with one's live recordings. Music performance is a unique moment in time that isn't re-created again, ever—so make use of this. On one hand, this is mostly due to the fact that artists understandably are concerned about both audio quality and are hard on themselves when listening to their own performances. On the other, the Grateful Dead have been doing this successfully for decades. So have a think on this, and I encourage you to take a whack at seeing if you can record your shows and share snippets or full shows with those who want the recordings and/or attended. A live show's recording is a special memento that people do want and is something that can now happen both due to technology and artists often owning their recording rights. As in the past, labels didn't want these live recordings to "compete" with studio albums and had the legal right to block such an idea. This is something you can set up on your own, or companies like Set.fm[26] will help you. If you own your rights, you can do a proper release of live recordings or just share to engage with your loyal Patreon subscribers. And always check with the venue before you release any recording from their room. At the same time, if you offer your recordings up for donation only, you might be able

---

26 https://set.fm/

to avoid the venue charging a fee, called an origination fee. As you are technically giving the content away and not selling it for a set price.

Your Daily Email and Text List Reminder

I want to reinforce how important it is for you to collect as many email addresses and text message subscribers on the road as possible. Again, you can offer fans a sticker or button/badge to incentivize them to sign up. And let whoever is selling your mech know—be it you, a group member, merch person you know, or a venue merch person—that when fans mull around the table, asking them to sign the email list is a great ice breaker.

As mentioned, your email list should be sturdy, say in a binder, and get creative with it so it looks good. It should be as essential to your gear bag as anything you need to perform with onstage. Similarly, don't forget to enter all of the email addresses you've collected at shows when you get home! Or even better, enter email addresses into your mailing list's database as you go while on tour, instead of letting it pile up. I see too many artists do the great work of collecting email addresses and then fail to put them into their email list program. Don't do all of the work without receiving the benefits! This is why Zoë Keating just puts out her text message list's subscribe number on posterboard in the venue's hallway - for ease of collection. Ideally, you want to do both.

CHAPTER 9:

MERCH RE-CON

We've already discussed merchandise or "merch" a bit through your preorder and live show strategies. But let's do a deeper dive to get creative while staying efficient and expanding your merchandise online.

Creation

Before you begin, give yourself about a month to produce merch, so you can go back and forth on artwork and production. That said, many artists begin creating merchandise before anyone even tells them to do so. Most know how to find a local T-shirt shop, if you want to go that route. I encourage you to start simple, as you'll have to pay for any physical goods up front. This can be as easy, but meaningful, as handwritten lyrics. However, let's, as always, start at the beginning.

First, your music should already be available through your website as downloads, CDs, and vinyl, so that's a great start. For good measure, you can also link to your preferred streaming platform to not miss a single fan. This can be anywhere on your site, but I'd put it on your merchandise page as well, so everything is in one place. I'd put Spotify, but know that Apple Music pays the highest streaming royalty rate as of this writing, so you could list them both and note that. I don't think you need to list all of the 150 plus digital service providers, or "DSPs," where your music is currently available. I don't even think you need list more than Spotify or Apple. But if you prefer Amazon, Tidal, or YouTube Music, go for it. It's not that we don't want to make this easy for your fans. It's more so that we don't want unnecessary clutter that distracts fans on your page; so use your best judgement.

If you have no or little budget, now is the time to use your creative skills. As mentioned, you can create handwritten lyrics; write a personal letter to fans; bake them cookies if you are paleo or vegan; offer to write a song (charge a lot for this); do a dedication shout-out via video or audio for a birthday, graduation, anniversary or special day; or create a custom voicemail message. The sky is really the limit here.

Many local print shops will help you create stickers and buttons/badges, and if you really want to get into it, you can buy a button/badge maker. Posters are a really cheap item that you can offer, and you can also charge more if the poster is autographed and even more if it's personally autographed. There are countless online and local T-shirt options as well, if that is of interest. Many artists opt to print in the United States or in countries that pay a fair wage. If you do so, note this publicly. Because if this is important to you, it's probably important to your fans as well. Also ask the print shop you're working with if you can provide the raw goods, as they will mark up any raw goods a bit, so that extra step can save you some cash.

Keep shipping and packaging materials in mind as well, as awkward or large items can be difficult to ship. For example, the cost of both printing and shipping a poster larger than eleven by seventeen is higher. Your profit margin is then diminished substantially, which should not be the case with something as simple as a poster.

With T-shirts, you'll be given a variety of price options. Think of what you want as a fan and consumer. Certainly not something itchy that will shrink or fall apart. But maybe you can't afford high-end designer Ts either. Ask the print shop you're working with what they recommend for a happy medium. Alternative Apparel is a great option that has a nice feel that fans tend to know and like. Also be mindful of how many colors you are using. Friends at merch companies have told me they always feel bad when a new artist is excited about a design, only to realize how expensive it is to print with five plus colors. Remember that you can have sleek and awesome merch with a more simplified design.

Similarly, when ordering any merchandise, including vinyl, ask where the price breaks are so you can make smart decisions and keep some stock for your live shows and on hand for your web store. Hopefully you've recouped many of your merch costs already with your preorder, making online and tour merch sales pure profit.

Shipping/Fulfillment

You're going to want to fulfill your orders or have a friend or eager and responsible fan do so as long as possible. Definitely compensate the person who is helping you if you're not fulfilling on your own. I've seen such fulfillment charges anywhere from one dollar per item to 5 percent of net. That's up to you.

Many artists get to know their local post office quite well for regular shipments. If you have a printer, you can also utilize Stamps.com to handle all fulfillment without ever leaving the house. Any sort of big box retailer (Target, etc.) will have bulk shipping materials, and you can also score whatever you need on Amazon.com.

Merch Companies/Physical Goods

When your merchandise orders get to be too much for any one human to handle, it's time to upgrade to a merch company. We like AKT in Florida and JSR in New Hampshire and know that there are a slew of great companies out there. Bandwear and Futureshirts both have excellent dashboards for real-time information. Bandwear in particular can sell your merchandise on Spotify and has a strong reputation across the board with what can feel like infinite merchandise item options. Everpress[27] is a company that will help you with merch on-demand as well. More traditional merch companies handling your webstore and fulfillment will receive a 20 percent cut or fee on all goods sold. And always ask your merch company to share fans' email addresses with you, and then ask the fans if it's OK for you to add them to your email list.

When your career grows and you have the cashflow to create new items, that is the time to truly go nuts with your merch. You can do hats, scarves, marijuana paraphernalia, long-sleeve shirts and hoodies, bandanas, beanies, temporary tattoos, patches, lighters, socks, phone cases, pens, backpacks, keychains, sunglasses—whatever you want. I personally think that there are way too many tote bags in the world, but that is up to you! I recently got rid of dozens that have piled up over the past few years, but if it's an item that speaks to you, absolutely go for it. Though maybe think twice on lighters, as they are full of butane, and anything flammable can be a pain to fulfill and costs extra. Also know that shipping alcohol to different states in particular is rather cumbersome legally, so I advise against it. And if you are doing something limited edition, be sure that the merch company lists this important detail on your webstore and give them explicit instructions.

When you really go big, for example with a signed piece of custom gear such as a guitar, make sure you send it with insurance. Also ensure that the packaging is done by a professional or that it is packaged in a manner that you know will get the gear there intact. If you cut costs on such an item, you and the fan might lose out in the end.

---

27 www.everpress.com

International Merch Companies

As your career grows beyond your own borders and you begin to tour internationally, you're going to want to print and ship in the continents you're touring in to save on shipping costs. Almost all merchandise companies have international partners, so ask who they recommend. Through JSR, we have worked with Firebrand for the UK, as well as a variety of companies (though just one at a time) to handle Europe, and definitely do the same for Australia, Asia, South America, Africa, and wherever you are touring.

Sales/Specials and Promotion

Everyone loves sales and special items for the holidays! So keep that in mind for Black Friday, the Fourth of July, the end of year holidays, and even your birthday They're your fans, so why not give them a reason to celebrate you? Again, get creative here with discount codes, special items, and Black Friday/holiday-only exclusive items and discounts. These discounts will earn you more money in the long run, increase fan engagement, and help spread the word on you.

Other than that, don't forget to promote your store in general! If it's just sitting on your website, few will notice. Push it out to your email / text lists and social media followers once it's live, and give your Patreon followers a discount. And promote your sales and specials upwards of once a month, as those are great talking points to re-highlight your merch store.

CHAPTER 10:

REVENUE STREAM CHECKLIST

Congratulations! You now know all elements of how to build a sustainable music career. However, it's not really sustainable if you're not collecting on all of your revenue streams. Upon this writing, I'd relatively recently began managing two national acts. One of which is known for her DIY prowess and is held up on a pedestal by the modern music industry as an example of how all artists should operate. What was disappointing to me for both artists, and stunning in the DIY darling's case, was that I very quickly kept finding revenue for them that was missing or that they were otherwise owed.

To be clear, I'm not necessarily talking about pre-digital revenue when artists had no control over owning their recording rights, resulting in situations such as:

XTC ✔️
@xtcfans

Do you know, I have absolutely NO IDEA how many albums XTC sold over the years. Record companies never tell you, as then they would have to pay you. Millions of albums? Sure, but how many? What territories?
Many times I asked Virgin, Cooking vinyl, TVT, they never will tell you.

10:55 PM - 14 Dec 2018

Though note that what Andy Partridge has stated defies the contract that he or any artist signed in the pre-digital era, a scenario that we will address in this chapter.

I was equally disheartened when one of the artists I had recently taken on told me that a reputable modern music company *called* to let her know they were sending a five-figure check. No statement, no quarterly payments per the agreement she had signed. This was from a company I know well that prides itself on artists owning their recording rights. But what's the point of owning your rights if you're not getting paid regularly? I contacted the company only to find out that the artist was currently owed a few thousand dollars more. Maybe that's nothing to the company. But not only is it two months of living expenses for the artist, it can also be used to wrap up and promote the music she's currently making. Not to mention that the agreement she signed lays out that she is owed regular statements and payments.

Just this morning of this writing, I saw an email from one of my co-managers on a third artist sent to a label saying:

Hi [Name],

Not sure if we ever received Q1–2 statements for this year.

Please advise! Thank you.

Best,

[Name]

I get that everyone is busy, but know that you are entitled to statements sent regularly per the terms you agreed to for any label or distribution company—if you are owed money or not. Even companies like Tunecore will hold onto money owed to artists/rights holders until you tell them you want to get paid.

And no offense to business managers, who we will discuss in chapter 12, but all of the artists I've alluded to in this chapter had or have business managers. At the end of the day, it is on you and to your benefit, no matter who you work with, to understand where your money is coming from as well as when it is coming.

I say all this not to create mistrust with your music partners, as they will pay you if you ask them. But to teach you how to get paid regularly - ensuring that you are collecting on all revenue streams and not missing any income or information.

Additionally, I'll show you how you can project and plan for future revenue streams. By doing this, you can then live knowing roughly when and how much you'll be paid moving forward, so you can plan accordingly. Almost kind of like how a "real" job works.

Let me preface this by saying that getting organized might be a little cumbersome and painful at first. Again, we're talking about an industry that was initially set up to confuse artists. But follow all steps, and I promise you'll get through it. By doing so, you'll be much more organized moving forward and know how to add new revenue streams seamlessly as you continue to grow your career. Here we go!

Revenue Stream Chart

For the aforementioned artists where I was finding revenue left and right, I ended up putting together a revenue stream chart so we could ensure nothing was missed and properly estimate financial projections moving forward.

Here is a blank version of that revenue stream chart, just for you: http://bit.ly/AllRevStreams (please note this URL is case-sensitive).

You can download this spreadsheet as a Microsoft Excel spreadsheet. And if you are like me and Microsoft products aren't your thing, you can then re-upload the file into Google Drive to create your own version. Here are the steps to enter your music revenue information:

Traditional Digital Distribution (i.e., Spotify, Tidal, Apple Music, etc.)

1. Begin by filling in every album, EP, or track you've ever released in column A on the first tab, in chronological order, under TITLE. Note that I've also put in a live recording session example from a blog called The Wild Honey Pie, as well as songs released as stand-alone singles as examples. You're going to want to put your entire catalog in here, including live sessions that have been released and pay you, such as The Wild Honey Pie example. In Column B, fill in how that album was distributed, for example, via CD Baby, Tunecore, a distributor, or a label. In Column C, note where the album is available via a direct to consumer

platform. This can be your website, and/or Bandcamp. If I've put in more rows than you have releases, clear the example title name(s) in column A, as well as unnecessary example data in columns B and C, to stay organized. Similarly, you can utilize the same steps to add rows if you need additional lines for your catalog.[28]

2.   I know this next step is a pain, but after much testing, we feel that it's necessary to allow each revenue stream its own tab and save you a lot of extra scrolling to get the information you need in an easy manner. (Note that if you added more rows for additional releases, you'll want to click on the DIGITAL DISTRIBUTION and DIRECT TO FAN DISTRIBUTION tabs to create more rows for your catalog there as well before proceeding). Therefore, I'd like for you to select cells 1 and 2 in Columns A and B. For the example I'm providing below, I'm selecting through A9:

---

28 You can add rows by clicking on the number on the far left hand side of the spreadsheet where you want to add a row, which will then highlight the entire row. From there, in Google Drive, click on "Insert" in the navigation bar up top, and select "Row above" or "Row below," depending on your desired row placement.

Revenue Stream Chart EXAMPLE `.XLSX` ☆ ■

File Edit View Insert Format Data Tools Help All ch₂

↶ ↷ 🖶 🖸 100% ▼ $ % .0 .00 123▼ Default (Ca... ▼

fx | TITLE

	A	B
1	TITLE	DIGITAL DISTRIBUTION
2	Album 1	CD Baby
3	Album 2	Indie label 1
4	Album 3	Tunecore
5	The Wild Honey Pie "Buzzsession" live release	Wild Honey Pie
6	Single 1	CD Baby
7	Single 2	CD Baby
8	Single 3	CD Baby
9	Single 4	CD Baby
10		
11		
12		
13	SUBTOTAL:	$ -
14	MONTHLY AVERAGE INCOME:	$ -
15	ANNUAL AVEAGE INCOME:	$ -
16		
17	TOTAL MONTHLY INCOME	$ -
18	TOTAL ANNUAL INCOME	$ -

From there, "copy" all of the cells you have selected, by pressing the command button and the c button at the same time on a Macintosh computer, or clicking on Edit in the navigation bar with the text selected, and choosing "copy." Then select cell A1, or TITLE, on the second tab of the spreadsheet, labeled DIGITAL DISTRIBUTION, as highlighted here:

Revenue Stream Chart .XLSX

File   Edit   View   Insert   Format   Data   Tools

100%   ▾ $ %   .0   .00   123▾

fx | TITLE

	A	DIGITAL
1	TITLE	DIGITAL
2	Album 1	CD Baby
3	Album 2	Indie lab
4	Album 3	Tunecore
5	The Wild Honey Pie "Buzzsession" live release	Wild Hor
6	Single 1	CD Baby
7	Single 2	CD Baby
8	Single 3	CD Baby
9	Single 4	CD Baby
10		
11		
12		
13	SUBTOTAL:	

Then press the command button and the letter "v" at the same time on Apple computers to paste your catalog into this column accordingly. Or click on Edit in the navigation bar up top and select Paste. Delete any data in cells that reference additional example releases to keep things organized. You can also double click the lines in between the column letter headers (A, B, etc.) to automatically shrink and resize each column accordingly. Your catalog will then be listed in full on the DIGITAL DISTRIBUTION tab ala:

	A	B
	Revenue Stream Chart EXAMPLE .XLSX	
	File Edit View Insert Format Data Tools Help All	
1	**TITLE**	**DIGITAL DISTRIBUTION**
2	Album 1	CD Baby
3	Album 2	Indie label 1
4	Album 3	Tunecore
5	The Wild Honey Pie "Buzzsession" live release	Wild Honey Pie
6	Single 1	CD Baby
7	Single 2	CD Baby
8	Single 3	CD Baby

Continue to "Paste" your title and direct to fan platform data from Columns A and C only from the first tab of the spreadsheet into Columns A and B on tab three of the spreadsheet titled DIRECT TO FAN DISTRIBUTION. You can do this by highlighting cells A1 through how many releases you have in Column A and copying the data, then clicking on cell A1 of the DIRECT TO FAN DISTRIBUTION and pasting the information there. Do the same for Column C from tab one of the spreadsheet titled Monthly & Annual Income Summary to get the data into Column B of DIRECT TO FAN DISTRIBUTION. Delete any data entry listed in cells as examples to keep things streamlined and organized.

3. Navigate over to the second tab in the spreadsheet, titled DIGITAL DISTRIBUTION. Here you can fill in your last payment amount from each release in column C. If you haven't received payment, ask your distributor or label for this information. As if there is income from your

recordings and you notice that you have empty cells here, you are missing income for that recording's release. And if there isn't yet income on that recording's release, find out how unrecouped you are if a distributor or label gave you an advance, to estimate when you will begin receiving royalties. For example, one of the artists I did this for has an album that was generating income, but the album is unrecouped. However, based on the album's income history, it is estimated to recoup on their next statement, and we can now plan for that accordingly.

4. Note the date of the statement you are entering financial data for in column D.

5. Note your future payment dates in column E.

6. Plug in how you get paid in column F. As you'll see, if you are using Tunecore, *you must log in to pay yourself.* Otherwise you will not receive any funds. However you go about reminding yourself to do anything—say, via Google Calendar alerts—set reminders for yourself to log into Tunecore on a regular basis and pay yourself out.

7. Note that I have entered projected formulas to calculate your monthly and annual incomes based on the example distribution partners' terms. For example, since CD Baby pays out weekly, the formula is inputted to multiply that income by four to estimate your monthly income for this revenue source. As the second example is payment from a label, which is often quarterly, I've entered a formula to divide your payment by 3, so you can project monthly income from this source. Please adjust these formulas accordingly per your individual payment terms. If you have added rows, make sure you adjust the formulas in the

SUBTOTAL rows in tabs 2 (DIGITAL DISTRIBUTION) and 3 (DIRECT TO FAN DISTRIBUTION). This is so they include the row numbers you have added to ensure all revenue is included. For example, if you've added one row, you'll need to adjust the formula in what is now the SUBTOTAL cells in C14 on both the DIGITAL DISTRIBUTION and DIRECT TO FAN DISTRIBUTION tabs. Thus, the formulas are then adjusted to =SUM(C2:C10), as opposed to =SUM(C2:C9) in the template version of the spreadsheet. If you add two rows for additional releases, your SUBTOTAL cells on the second and third tabs of the spreadsheet will then read =SUM(C2:C11), and so on. Once you have edited the formulas to your catalog's specific payment terms, you'll then see that your SUBTOTAL on the DIGITAL DISTRIBUTION tab of the spreadsheet is now updated to reflect an actual monetary amount. And when you navigate back over to the first tab on the spreadsheet, Monthly & Annual Income Summaries, that subtotal is also now reflected in Column B accordingly.

If you are totally overwhelmed by spreadsheet formulas, that's OK. But find someone in your life who can help you adjust these to your specific payout terms. One of the most useful classes I've ever taken was software applications my sophomore year of high school. Find someone with this level of spreadsheet education to help you. I guarantee you there is someone in your life that knows how to, and if not, there are countless free tutorials online and on YouTube. However, since many of your payouts will be quarterly, many of these formulas will hold true for you.

Direct-to-Fan Distribution

Next up, check to ensure that all of your releases have data entered in the third tab of the spreadsheet, titled DIRECT TO FAN DISTRIBUTION. This notes how each release is being distributed directly to fans (i.e., via your website, Bandcamp, and/or a label's website). Really, it should be all of the above if you are signed, but that will not necessarily be the case if you're using Bandcamp's tools to embed and sell music via your website. Again, if you are missing an entry here, you are missing out on revenue.

For example, when putting together this revenue spreadsheet for one of my artists, I noticed one of her label releases wasn't on Bandcamp. Unfortunately, as of this writing, the label has refused to release the album on Bandcamp, despite the fact that I have been asking labels to utilize Bandcamp in general since 2014 or so.[29] But the label says they will soon, and I've been told this by Bandcamp's founder as well. A true shame in the meantime. As after the artist was dropped from the label and she released her new song on Bandcamp, where fans could name their own price instead of being limited to streaming or $.99 on download stores, the average price each fan paid for the song was $8. If your label refuses to distribute on Bandcamp, point out that the platform has paid out upwards of a half billion US dollars to artists and rights holders to-date, as of this writing. If they don't see the light in that, you could also point out that Bandcamp shares email addresses for future marketing and sales. But in this instance these points got me nowhere, so, seriously, good luck.

---

29 Why (not) Bandcamp? [Emily White] via Hypebot: https://www.hypebot.com/hypebot/2014/11/why-not-bandcamp.html

Regardless, after a year of sales, you should be able to estimate monthly and annual income from your direct-to-fan revenue after it has tapered off from the initial release.

In the meantime, your subtotal on each tab, as well as the subtotals on the first page of the spreadsheet will now update accordingly.

Performing Rights Organizations (e.g., ASCAP, BMI, etc.)
Begin by filling in your last performing rights organization payments on tab 4, PRO (e.g. ASCAP, BMI, etc.). ASCAP, for example, actually pays the first two months of every quarter, but it's a different revenue stream you're receiving each month of the quarter. The first is your domestic writer's distribution. Your international distribution comes the second month of the quarter. Since your publishing share is collected by Songtrust or a publishing company, which we'll discuss next, you won't receive a payment for the third month of each quarter. I like that ASCAP does this, though, as they're trying to get you payments more frequently than just quarterly. Keeping with ASCAP just for the sake of example, if you signed up with direct deposit when you registered, there is no action required to get paid here. But again, *don't forget to register new songs as soon as you write them* so you don't miss a single cent moving forward.

Publishing
Column E and tab 5 titled PUBLISHING contains your publishing revenue. If publishing revenue comes in via Songtrust, this is very straightforward. If you have a publishing deal and recently received advances, put that information in instead. Keep this section updated with each

statement so you know when you will recoup and how much you can plan on bringing in every month after that.

If you click on the cells for *subtotal, monthly average,* and *annual total* in rows 4, 5, and 6, you'll see that I've put in suggested formulas. This is to estimate your monthly publishing income. Since Songtrust pays quarterly, I've divided these numbers by three, one for each month in the quarter. We then multiply your monthly average times twelve to generate your annual revenue for each column.

SoundExchange

Next up is your tab labeled SOUNDEXCHANGE, which will automatically pay you monthly via direct deposit if you're making more than $100 per month. If not, you'll receive quarterly checks. To receive a quarterly payment, you must have accrued at least $10 that quarter (or $100 for a paper check) in royalties before a scheduled distribution will be paid out. If you are under these limits, SoundExchange will hold your royalties until enough funds have accrued.

Again, I've put in suggested formulas in rows 4, 5, and 6 so you can estimate what you generate monthly and what you make annually from SoundExchange.

Patreon

Navigate over to the tab labeled PATREON / FAN CLUB. Set up your Patreon account to pay out monthly automatically for ease of receiving funds. Again, the formulas are in the revenue spreadsheet template I've provided. This is so you can then estimate your income from Patreon and project your annual payments moving forward for this category, as they average out the longer you are on the platform.

Online Merchandise

Next, click on the tab labeled ONLINE MERCH. If you are self-fulfilling, plug in your net revenue, which is the funds you're making after manufacturing and shipping. If working with a merchandise company, note the terms that you agreed to, which is usually the merch company sending you monthly statements. Some companies may require you to invoice for payment, and regardless, put their payment terms into your calendar alerts (or however you remind yourself about things in general) to ensure you receive them. And ask the company if you haven't received past statements so you can get that information, and remember to invoice for the funds that you are owed moving forward. Also ask for customer email addresses so you can ask those fans if they'd like to be added to your email list.

Live Revenue and Merchandise

On the tab labeled LIVE DATES, put in all of your tour dates as they arise. If there isn't a "guarantee" payment for each date, start to estimate what you'll earn based on past dates as they happen, so you can budget and plan. For months that you don't have any shows, do a monthly webcast show on StageIt. To entice and engage with your StageIt webcast fans further, offer them a discount code for the merch store for the next twenty-four hours. This is just like having a physical merch table (and revenue stream) at in-person live shows.

Also paste your dates on the tab labeled LIVE SHOW MERCH, along with inputting the costs to print and ship merchandise so you know the "cost of goods sold," or COGS, and can calculate your net revenue on live merch. This will help you to project what you'll make for future months and tours on live merchandise.

Bonus Revenue Streams

Here are more ways to generate income as a musician beyond what is owed to you for your recordings, songwriting, live performances and fan engagement. If you pursue any/all of the below, I've created a tab in your spreadsheet for these revenue sources called BONUS REVENUE STREAMS. We'll highlight some of these revenue stream options as follows.

VIP Experiences for Fans

We have a Julia Nunes tour going out shortly where fans can purchase a Soundcheck Party ticket upsell in addition to their regular ticket for the concert that evening. Most promoters have generously let us keep 100% of this additional income. Keep this in mind to enhance your audience's experience and your live revenue streams as your fanbase grows.

Live Recordings

I don't see this often, but I feel that artists can and should be recording their shows for content and revenue streams. You can do this on your own or work with companies like Set.fm for tools to do so.

Catalog Vinyl

If your past releases aren't on vinyl, launch a pre-order campaign to make that a reality. You can build in higher price points for autographed and personalized items, as mentioned throughout this book, and also do so sustainably by knowing how many pieces you need to order using your pre-order numbers. You can also use any remaining stock from the order, based on price break quantities you are close to hitting, for your live shows and online merch store. And for all of your vinyl releases, both new and catalog, drop a note to CIMS, or the Coalition of Independent Music Stores, to see if they'll buy vinyl directly from you to distribute to record shops.

Sheet Music

You might get requests for sheet music or guitar tabs from time to time. Think about taking this to the next level, as Amanda Palmer did for a Dresden Dolls' sheet music book. Amanda and Brian Viglione of The Dolls made a sheet music book so gorgeous, with photos and stories of the recording sessions, that it became a high-end merch item that was in demand from fans who couldn't or had no plans to ever read or play the music contained within.

Music Lessons

Teaching is one of life's greatest gifts, and I love that some of my favorite musicians offer music lessons. Here is a great shot of Brian Viglione (The Dresden Dolls, Nine Inch Nails, Violent Femmes, etc.) with one of his many drum students of all ages:

30

Don't overlook music lessons as a revenue stream, as it's also a fun way to give back to those who want to learn your skills.

Branding, Endorsement, Sponsorship, and Podcasting
If, to date, you've built a strong enough following that local or national brands want to partner with you to authentically endorse them, add this in. Same if you've scored a sponsor for your podcast or have grown enough regular podcast listeners that you're generating revenue through ad-based podcast distribution.

Speaking Engagements
As some of the musicians on our roster also do speaking engagements around the world, I would be remiss to omit speaking gigs as a potential revenue stream.

---

30 Photo courtesy of Brian Viglione.

This isn't for everyone, but I also feel that those who have the opportunity are fortunate, and this revenue category should not be overlooked. If you are starting to get offers to perform at colleges, see if you or your agent can negotiate a moderated Q&A while you're on campus, for an additional fee. This Q&A can be anything from a music workshop or master class to a talk about additional fields you are passionate about, such as say activism or mental health. Dessa is an example of an artist who generates strong speaking revenue. This payment can come from a school, brand, non-profit, or presenting campus group.

YouTube

Note that I did not have a spreadsheet tab for YouTube. If you own all of the rights to your content, have over 1,000 YouTube subscribers or 4,000 "valid public watch hours" over the last 12 months, you are eligible for YouTube's Partner Program for monetization. Whether you've hit these thresholds or not, if you own your master and video rights, please sign up for a third party content ID, or identification company, such as InDMusic. This is to ensure your recorded music and content is being fully monetized on YouTube, beyond what is already being collected on for any and all songwriting royalties you are owed.

But many folks do not make significant regular revenue from YouTube, and I wanted to keep the revenue spreadsheet as simple and straightforward as possible. That said, if you are making money on YouTube, please plug it in per the example I have started in the BONUS REVENUE STREAMS tab.

Synch Licenses

I have not put an entry into the spreadsheet for master and publishing licenses, since such placements are not guaranteed and are sporadic. This doesn't mean that there isn't significant revenue to be found here! Especially for those that own their master and/or publishing rights without an advance payment that these funds would otherwise go towards paying off. If you are landing synchs, absolutely add this in to the bonus revenue stream column and tab on your revenue spreadsheet. Although synch income should not be relied upon, as your career grows, you can start to estimate how much you'll receive annually, if you are receiving relatively consistent placements and own your rights or are debt-free with a partner.

Mixcloud

Mixcloud is a community of DJ's in which creators can now charge a fee to listen to live shows and more. If you are a DJ, absolutely check out the platform and begin monetizing. Then, add or overwrite a row for your Mixcloud revenue on the BONUS REVENUE STREAMS tab of your revenue spreadsheet per their terms and the rate that you set.

Playing and Working with Other Artists

As you now know how to compensate musicians, producers, and engineers that you hire, keep in mind ensuring that you get paid when you play on other artists' recordings, or session work, and shows. Also keep in mind producing, mixing, mastering, and remixing recordings for other artists while ensuring that you get properly compensated, which has been laid out in chapter 3 of this book. Same goes for arranging a song or songs for another artist.

Monthly and Annual Income

Once you have completed all of this, you can now calculate your average monthly and annual income! I've put in suggested formulas so your music's monthly and annual revenue totals are noted in cells B17 and B18 on the first tab of the example spreadsheet we have given you. Note that some revenue streams' monthly averages should be calculated after a year, as stated accordingly on the spreadsheet, to realistically project income over a longer period of time.

Hopefully, you can now estimate what you will make monthly and annually moving forward. You can also identify what revenue streams are the strongest, as well as examine those that you need to work on. And naturally, as you create more music, you'll have more new revenue for each available stream.

Again, *if there is a blank cell in any column or row of your spreadsheet, then you are missing revenue!* That has been the case with every artist I've ever taken on, so it's probably the same for you as well. I'm hoping to solve that for all moving forward with this chapter and book.

Neighboring Rights

One revenue stream that we did not cover in this book, or the aforementioned spreadsheet, is neighboring rights. The vast majority of countries outside the United States pay performers for public performance royalties on master recordings. What does this mean? Similar to when an artist gets paid in the US via their performing rights organization (e.g., ASCAP, BMI, etc.), the master recording side is the "neighbor" right to this revenue stream. Amazing organizations like Future of Music Coalition, whose board I've served on, do great advocacy work to change this policy in the United States so American recording artists can be compensated as well.

In the meantime, generally speaking—but please check your specific country, as laws can change—if you recorded your music outside of the

United States and are making money on the PRO side, you are owed royalties on the neighboring rights side. There isn't a "do it yourself" way to collect this revenue yet, so in the meantime, if you are owed funds, we encourage you to work with companies such as Sentric and Premier. Know that collecting on neighboring rights takes a bit of paperwork with original signatures. This is not said to deter you but just to let you know that it's a little more legwork to obtain these royalties owed to you than all other revenue streams that we have laid out. If you are owed funds and follow these steps to collect, please add a row with, or overwrite, the financial information to add to your BONUS REVENUE STREAMS tab on the spreadsheet.

Revenue Stream Checklist

To recap, here are all revenue streams you should be collecting on as a recording artist who also writes at least some portion of their songs:

- Distribution

- Direct-to-fan digital distribution

- Performing rights organization (e.g., ASCAP, BMI, etc.)

- Publishing

- SoundExchange

- Patreon

- Online merchandise

- Live performances and webcasts

- Live merchandise

Furthermore, here are additional revenue streams to maximize your income as a musician:

- VIP live show offerings

- Live recordings

- Catalog releases on vinyl and CIMS distribution

- Sheet music

- Music lessons

- Podcast revenue

- Branding, sponsorships and endorsements

- Speaking engagements

- Synch licenses (if landed, you own your rights, and are not unrecouped to a label or publishing company).

- YouTube royalties

- Playing on other artists' recordings, or session work, and shows

- Producing, mixing, mastering, remixing other artists' recordings or arranging songs for other artists

Again, if you are not collecting revenue from any of the above categories, *you are missing revenue on your music.* So go and get it! And don't forget to add in new releases and live/paid promotional sessions to your revenue spreadsheet as you go.

I began working in music years ago because I loved it so much. I've always wanted to support artists because you're the reason music exists. I want you to survive and thrive, and all of the above is how you can keep creating the work that we all love and cherish deeply. And now it's time to keep going! The next chapter will explain how to grow from the release you followed the steps of this book on into a long-term career.

CHAPTER 11:

REPEAT AND GROW!

You did it! You made it through your first modern music release, which is also the first brick in building a sustainable music career. I followed these same steps for my first book, *Interning 101*, in which we *still* have elements that I can use to spread the word on it, even though the book was released years ago.

But like you, I've been also planting seeds for this very book you're reading. As some of you know, a pre-order was launched when I hit the halfway point of writing because I asked my publisher to follow a "recoup before release" business model. We are on track to not only do just that, but the direct-to-fan preorder through my company's website has already garnered more sales than what was sold *total* via direct-to-fan for my first book over the years.

Why? Because I followed my own advice. And now it's time for you to do the same. Hopefully, your promotion and live date cycle takes some time. Again, I still have Amazon reviews from my first book that I want to share on social media, as well as a few podcast episodes that bring the tenets of my previous book to life. Yet I also know it is time to wind down that project as the book you are reading comes to life. You'll know when things die down a bit, as well as when you're ripe to begin creating your next release. If you are like most artists, you're already clamoring to make more music. But first, give your project a moment to breathe to ensure you've followed every step in this book. When there are just a few elements left to promote, if any, and your art is together for your next release, it's time to begin the process again.

Like with anything, every time you go through each step, you'll learn the information in a deeper way. Eventually many, if not all, of these elements will become a habit. So it shouldn't feel daunting to go back to the beginning of this book. It should be akin to reviewing all of your work for the past semester. And when you've mastered it all, you're then ready to student teach others, eventually becoming a professor of your own career.

To recap, here is a checklist of the steps/chapters of this book as an overview for your next release:

1. **Get Your Art Together:** Remember, don't put the cart before the horse! I know you are excited, but that energy is wasted if your art isn't in the best possible place it can be before you put your recording plan together.

2. **Pre-recording Marketing Foundation - Email List, Text Message Club and Social Media:** Good news! Your email list and social media accounts are already in place. Now it's time to use these platforms to grow your foundation with the skills that you are constantly getting better at every day. Here are some suggestions on how to utilize these platforms, before you begin recording your next release:

    The Power of Email and Text: Send a blast to your loyal email/text list subscribers, thanking them for all of their support on your last release. Your career is nothing without them. Let them know that you are already putting plans in the works for your next release and that they will be the first to know about it.

<u>Patreon Update</u>: Let your equally loyal Patrons know that new music is coming soon. Offer to share a demo or video teaser to whet their appetites, as well as to thank them for their ongoing support. Let them know how much that support means to you.

<u>Social Media</u>: Post on your social media accounts, teasing your fans to stay tuned as creative plans are coming together for new music. Include links in these posts to your email and text lists so fans can stay in the loop on your new music directly. This way they don't miss any news posted on social media due to algorithms.

<u>Pre-Order Review</u>: Take a look back at your last pre-order campaign. What worked? What didn't? Where were your sales strongest? Are there any elements you should drop or revise? Learn from your previous experience and take that knowledge into the next release you are now planning. Prepare your next release's pre-order launch, ensuring that you get it out to your Patreon fans first, then your email/text list subscribers, and announce it on social media, pinning the news at the top of your pages. Add the news to your website too. And again, if you don't know what your next release will be, but you are commencing the creative process, let your Patreon fans know this so they can support you as it comes together into a cohesive project and plan.

3. **Get Your Business Affairs Together and Fair Compensation:** You will get more comfortable with this element on every release. As with all of the steps in this book, you are gaining more experience every day.

The Business of Recording: Sort out how you are going to pay your players in advance. Think about if you're going to work with the same producer or if you're going to try someone new. There's certainly no right or wrong answer here, as you know what best speaks to your creative vision. Similarly, sort out how the producer will be compensated in advance. And in the least, put these terms into an email that you both agree to if a legal agreement isn't currently in the budget. My lawyer friends won't like that, but I'm also trying to be realistic as far as the next best option when there aren't funds for a proper legal agreement.

Work for Hires: Do not pay anyone, including the players, producer, or have anyone who has walked into the studio leave, without a signed work for hire agreement that you will provide for them. This is available via a variety of options online. Pay half of their rate up front and half once the work has been finished and you receive a signed work for hire form. This is standard, as it incentivizes everyone to prioritize the project and wrap up, and also ensures that your producer delivers the masters and instrumentals. If you are sharing favors with players, and playing on their recording in return, you should each sign a work for hire for each other's projects as well.

Real Songwriting Splits: Have a group conversation with your players and producers on songwriting *before* you enter the studio. If you have written all of the songs, let the group know that if they feel they have written something in the studio, they need to bring it up in the moment or immediately following the session to avoid any issues later. And reminder: arranging or remixing is not songwriting.

4. **How to Record with or without a Budget:** Decide how much you want to spend on recording based on what options are available and what you are going for creatively. Start to think about artwork for your release at this stage as well. And make sure anyone who does artwork for or with you also signs a work for hire agreement.

5. **Collect on Your Music Publishing:** Follow the steps below to ensure you are collecting the funds owed to you for your songwriting.

> Register New Songs With Your PRO: Assuming you have already registered for your performing rights organization (PRO) of choice, after you finish recording, immediately register your new songs with your PRO (e.g., ASCAP, BMI, etc.).

> Publishing Administration Collection: If working with Songtrust to collect on your music publishing, log into your account to register your new songs there as well. If you have a music publisher, email them the new song titles and songwriting splits and ask them to confirm receipt of the email. Also include download links to WAV files of your masters, WAV files of your instrumentals, high-quality MP3 links to your songs and instrumentals, as well as Spotify links to your new material as soon as it is available there. Additionally include the lyrics to your new music as a PDF attachment. And make sure that you get a response to said email.

6. **How to Increase Your Chances of Landing Synch Placements:** Follow the basic steps below to make your synch pitching company's days and life easier, to increase your chances of standing out and landing music in films, television, web shows and advertisements.

Ease of Delivery: If you are working with a third-party synch placement company, in addition to your publisher, send a similar email as to what is outlined above, delivering your new music in an organized manner to your synch-pitching person.

Mindfully Inform and Engage: Keep *both* your synch-pitching company and publisher in the loop on your release plans, live dates, and any press or radio action that comes in. Remind them that you're always happy to put them or anyone they want on your shows' guest lists. Do so no more than once or twice a month, when there is news to share, and try to reach out at the top of the week; not on nights, weekends, or holidays.

7. **Setting Up Your Release and Distribution Plans:** Below is a recap based on your particular situation to strategize getting your music out as far as possible, while retaining as much data for your own future use as you can.

    PR: If working with a publicist, let them know that you are setting up your release plan and ask what their ideal time period is for release. Ensure that it does not conflict with any major holidays.

    Digital Distribution: Did your previous release bring in more than $555.44 USD + Tunecore's fee (which varies depending on if it's a single, album, etc.) a year via digital service providers such as Spotify? If so, you should work with Tunecore for the best profit margin on your new release. If not, stick with CD Baby, Label Engine, or check out Level. If a distribution company beyond the aforementioned "aggregators" or a label is interested, consider those options as well for your digital distribution partner, keeping your rights and all percentages laid out in this book in mind for reference.

Direct to Fan: Once you've set a release date, get your music uploaded to Bandcamp so you can do an additional pre-order there if you'd like. Though you're ideally going to want to be pushing everyone to the pre-order that you own and control through your website, to receive the highest sales margins possible. This is where you want to be selling your higher-end items and price points, as Bandcamp currently has financial limits on price points and you'll keep a larger share of sales revenue through your website. Either way, Bandcamp shares email addresses with you, so let your fans know that your website and Bandcamp are the best ways for people to support your music purchases directly.

Physical Distribution: Think about if you are doing enough vinyl and CD sales to warrant physical distribution. Don't be bummed if you aren't; plenty of artists you've heard of do not fall into this category. The Coalition of Independent Music Stores will let you know demand on their end regarding vinyl. Use your pre-order to dictate if CD distribution is warranted. I manage an artist who just sold over one thousand CDs via Kickstarter, and most indie distributors passed on the option to distribute her CDs. Therefore, don't be disappointed if physical distribution doesn't make sense for you.

8. **Marketing Your Release:** Now that your release plan is in place, it's time to make sure you're communicating this news to your fanbase and beyond with the following steps.

<u>Focus on Your Own Green Grass</u>: Take a deep breath. Focus on yourself while also helping others. This is how you move forward—not by bemoaning others' Instagram posts, wondering why you don't have what they have. Social media is literally programmed to result in FOMO[31], and know that those you are looking at have "the grass is always greener" feelings too. Not to mention that people likely feel that way about you as well! If you truly can't stand it, reach out to connect with the artists you are admiring to see if they're up to share some advice. But know that anyone who "makes it" without being true to their own creative spirit won't make it in the long-term.

<u>Finding Balance</u>: Set limits on your social media and email time so you don't get lost in marketing, as you are an artist at the end of the day. A savvy artist! But know that commerce won't happen without great art.

<u>Email List, Text Club, and Patreon</u>: Prepare an announcement for your email and text list subscribers to share information on when your release will be out. Aim to send it out the day of release for instant gratification. Give your Patreon followers a day or so heads up, as they deserve the news early for supporting you throughout the process.

<u>Music Platform Announcements</u>: Announce when your release is live on Spotify, Apple, Tidal, Audiomack, and other major platforms on your social media. Pin your direct to fan and/or Bandcamp release announcement at the top of your social media pages, as Bandcamp is the platform (outside of your website) where you will gain the most revenue. Bandcamp will also let you know who your

---

31 "Fear of missing out"

fans are, since they share fan email addresses with artists and rights holders.

Engage and Grow: Engage with your audience and followers, getting back to everyone who is supporting you. Make additional announcements if your release goes live on some platforms later than others. This gives you more excuses to promote your work on your social media. And always tag every noun that you can—music platforms, journalists, media outlets writing about you, etc. Review Ariel Hyatt's latest tips to score Spotify and streaming platform playlists, shouting those out when landed. Decide if it benefits your music, based on what genres you are in, to upload your music to Soundcloud.

Consider PR and Radio: Review chapter 7 if you are working with a publicist and/or are considering radio promotion to ensure the left hand is talking to the right with regard to cohesive promotion.

9. **Live Strategy and Efficient Touring:** When it's time to start playing out, you want to do so with a plan in place per the following steps.

Practice Makes Perfect: Get your live act together before playing out.

Hometown Love, Booking a Show 101, Metrics, and Regional Touring: Review the strategies laid out in chapter 8 until these best practices become second nature. *Always* have an email/text club list out and consider it as important as a piece of gear for your shows. Let metrics guide where you play, setting up gig swaps with artists in other cities whenever you can. Make sure you have a

Square reader on hand at all live performances to accept credit / debit card sales at the merch table, as well as to collect additional fan email addresses for your list.

House Shows and Webcasts: Consider safely booking house shows through reputable companies to connect with fans, and do a webcast a month or so, whether you can hit the road or not.

How to Land Support Tours: Build a community and genuinely make friends with other artists. If your goal is to have an agent, know that you're going to have to focus on building up your hard ticket count shows regionally, not just in your home base. However, a killer local draw is a great start, as it can lead to you supporting national/international acts when they come through your town, as well as setting up the aforementioned gig swaps to grow your fanbase outside your home market.

Maximizing Tour Profits: Consider holding off on every bell and whistle available on the road as you grow, so you come home with as much money as possible. You can also re-invest these saved funds back into your career if you'd like, so you can keep growing and making music instead of blowing it all on one tour. Think about recording your shows and getting creative with these recordings. And don't forget to import the email addresses you collect at shows into your email list's database.

10. **Merch-Land:** Just as you reviewed your last pre-order, take a look at what has worked for you with your online merch sales and what hasn't, to see if you can come up with some new items to excite your fans for this release. Consider a sale to sell off any old stock from your last release for Black Friday and holidays.

11. Collect All Revenue Streams: Update your revenue spreadsheet with your new release, ensuring that all columns are filled, as if not, you're missing money. So go get it if that's the case!

And that brings us up to date! Follow the steps in this book for each and every release to build and grow a sustainable career. The tools are out there to do so; now it's on you to create great art and utilize these tools to do just that.

But what happens when it all truly becomes too much to do? There are only so many hours in the day. Know that this is different from not *wanting* to do all of the above. The next chapter will outline the roles of traditional music industry team members who may or may not enter your career at any stage of the process. Regardless, you're going to want to adhere to everything you've learned in this book to build and sustain a long-term career. This is because industry professionals are human too and may come or go for a variety of reasons. At the end of the day, it's on you to know who your fans are and where your money is coming from.

CHAPTER 12:

WHEN DO I NEED AN ATTORNEY, A BUSINESS MANAGER, AND/OR A MANAGER?: DEFINING AN ARTIST'S TRADITIONAL "TEAM"

How are you feeling? Hopefully fully informed and ready to go. However, one topic I rarely touch on throughout this book of building a sustainable career is that of building an industry team. Many of us at the forefront of the modern music industry see all of the tools that are now available to artists as replacing elements that were necessary for a career in the pre-digital era. In particular, recording, distribution, and direct to fan engagement. This certainly doesn't mean having industry professionals involved in your career is not an asset. At the same time, know that many people in the music industry have had to educate themselves on everything that we've covered and are often still educating themselves to understand the "new" music industry.

As discussed, music industry entities that artists often have the least amount of access to, like major labels, are *looking* for you to have mastered everything covered in this book before they consider signing you. This includes making great art, but now more than ever, that isn't necessarily enough. If you aren't putting the work and effort into your career, in particular with regard to growing your fanbase, why should anyone else?

That said, there is great value to working with experienced professionals, and most artists want a team. Again, it is to your benefit to understand the tenets of this book even when you have a team. Either way, in this chapter, I'm going to cover the various members of an artist's traditional team so you have an understanding of their roles.

Attorney

I'm starting here not because I feel that attorneys are the most important people on your team. No offense to the truly incredible souls in my life who also happen to be attorneys. I'm bringing this up first because often when I meet new artists, an attorney seems to be the one team member that they have on board. Again, there are fantastic human beings out there who also happen to be attorneys. But the reason so many artists have an attorney as their first industry team member, is that you're more often than not, paying them cash up front. Because of this, I recommend thinking about whether an attorney is really necessary as your first team member. I feel that you should work with an attorney any time someone offers you a significant agreement—not limited to contracts regarding a producer, label, publisher, or manager. Everything else covered in this book is rather standard as far as terms go (say, CD Baby and Tunecore's prices, for example). Many attorneys from the pre-digital era aren't wrong to let you know that they'll "shop" your music to labels. But again, that was more useful when you needed a label to record and distribute. Now this is not your only option for the world to hear your music.

Attorneys generally charge anywhere from $300 to $750 per hour with a retainer up front of, say, $1,500 to $2,500. Some also work on a 5 percent commission of your earnings, similar to a manager, but at a lower rate than a manager's commission.

When the time does come to hire a lawyer, please get a music attorney! You might think you're saving money by having your family's real estate attorney review your publishing agreement. This will not only hurt you in the long run, but you're also going to come off as an amateur. And it may cost you more in the short-term, since said real estate attorney will need more time to figure out the nuances of a field they do not work in. Again, the music industry was set up decades ago to confuse artists, so know that an attorney who doesn't work in music is going to be in over their head almost immediately. If possible, get a true music attorney, not even a firm that does "entertainment" and sometimes does music. You're paying for an expert and therefore deserve real expertise on your agreements.

Manager

Up next is arguably your most crucial team member, though to be fair, I'm most likely biased in saying so as a long-time manager. At the same time, I feel that one of the most challenging elements of being a manager is that whether you realize it or not, you probably have an idea in your mind of what a manager might be like and what they might do for you and your career. Frankly, these expectations in one's mind can be super frustrating in reality, as we managers are human beings, not miracle workers. So much so that when people ask me the difference between managing musicians and athletes, I tell them that athletes don't grow up with an idea in their head of what their manager will be like. They just happen to be incredible at their craft. To counter this, my business partner Melissa Garcia always asks a brilliant question when we are deciding whether to take a client on or not: Have they had management before us? If the answer is no, it's most likely a pass for her. This is because we can never live up to the expectations built up in an artist's mind. If yes, that is attractive to us. As not only do we have a deep belief in our skills as managers, but the artist has some experience working with managers and hopefully understands that we are humans too; which I will elaborate on.

But before I do, the qualities I personally look for in artists is threefold: 1. Do I love their art? 2. I don't want to work harder than they do. 3. We don't work with assholes, no matter their talent or earnings. That's just me. I know others that are OK working with jerks, who could care less about the art if they see commercial potential. Or who will consider working with an artist only if their live show is incredible and they're committed to touring. There are plenty of talent managers with clients who do not perform live, such as producers and songwriters. So if this is the camp you fall into, don't be discouraged. And know that even if your manager is willing to put up with asshole-esque behavior, many others in the industry will not, and this will hurt your career in the long run.

What exactly is a manager? A manager sets short- and long-term goals with the artist and assembles or inherits a team around the artist (often making changes along the way, always with artist approval), ensuring that the team is working hard and diligently toward those short- and long-term goals. As the industry has evolved into the post-digital era, the manager's role has evolved to often running a variety of elements that we didn't handle previously, not limited to music distribution and promotion. More often than not, managers are essentially taking on the role of a label, working on a variety of elements for an artist's career that used to be handled by teams of people. So be nice to us!

I'm serious. Just like I try to empathize with what it's like on the other end of the phone, Slack, and inbox for you, as well as everyone I engage with on your behalf, it's going to help if you do the same. At this stage in my career, I've tried to put some limits on my time, such as wrapping up work by a reasonable hour and taking my weekends off. Obviously if something arises, I'm going to deal with it, and our work does spill into weekends and holidays in the live sector. That's OK. But if you're asking for something on a Friday afternoon and following up on a Monday to ask if your manager has heard back from someone yet, you're wasting your manager's time and energy. Time that could otherwise be spent moving your career forward.

Despite all of this, management is interesting because it touches all aspects of an artist's career. Yet it is a role in the industry that does not require a degree, license, or any sort of formal training. This results in countless "friend-agers," "parent-agers," "fan-agers," and even sycophants. (Watch the film *All About Eve* if you want to learn what a sycophant is.) Many of these folks, excluding the sycophant category, go on to be incredible talent managers. Although Beyoncé has since moved on, and he was clearly very intense, I do feel that B appreciates her father's management of her career and that of Destiny's Child. The Jackson family? Probably not so much.

Regardless, you want someone who is passionate about your career and is interested in building a career in the music industry and isn't just obsessed with you. Although having someone who lives and breathes for your existence sounds great, it isn't good for you or your career. Whether it's a family member or a fan, if they are so focused on you, they will lack the perspective to understand the bigger picture of your career and the industry at large. And most likely stomp all over relationships that could otherwise potentially help you. Therefore, look for balance in a manager. They're most likely not going to take you on if they don't believe in you. And you want someone who works hard. But working hard also requires rest and balance, which does not necessarily mean being available twenty-four/seven.

Similarly, if you come across someone who is both passionate about you and your career and wants to build a career in the industry because they love music, do not overlook them. That was me! I began working with The Dresden Dolls in college, as mentioned. It was to both of our benefits that we connected and became a part of each other's worlds. We essentially grew up professionally together. The band had other offers of help from fans, and I was a fan. But when I initially introduced myself to Amanda Palmer at the merchandise table after the band played a show at my school, I did so professionally. I told her I was a music industry major at the university and interned at a nearby radio station and wrote for a local music magazine. I asked her to let me know if she ever needs help with anything. I was super nervous to ask that question, yet her response was, "Can you come over tomorrow?"

A year or so later, the band had grown, and a slew of managers were interested in them. I'm forever grateful that they went with Mike Luba, who instantly incorporated me into the team, instead of others who I feel may have been threatened by my presence. You want to work with people that put you and the greater good of the work, not their own personal egos, first. That's Luba to a T. Regardless, managers should never do anything without your permission, no matter their level. This also empowers you to take on someone like me—a college student who believes in you, is up to work hard, yet is also on a professional path. As long as they don't do anything sans permission, then you are truly a team and partnership.

Still, this question comes up often: When does an artist "need" a manager? I feel that one "needs" a manager when they've done everything in this book and their careers have gotten to a level where they truly can no longer handle the workload. Which is different from not wanting to do the work.

Managers generally receive a 15 percent gross commission on all aspects of an artist's career, though there can be deductions for merchandise costs and other elements that can be negotiated. That said, many managers are OK with half commission on gross merchandise numbers to save time in making the extra deductions and calculations pertaining to cost of goods sold. In the UK, managers are often paid 20 percent of all net revenue. These numbers generally come out to be roughly the same between US and UK managers. Some managers accept a salary in the early days of an artist's career, but more often than not, they work on commission. Managers can also work on salary at the highest levels of superstar artists.

Generally managers sign artists for a set amount of years, or a term. However, I do not sign artists to a term length, as I feel that either party should be able to leave at any time, without being forced to work together. Regardless, managers are traditionally entitled to a diminishing "post-term" commission on works they were involved in, should a split occur. I set what my attorney calls a "mirrored term," in which managers at our company receive diminishing post-term commissions for as long as we worked with an artist. So if we worked with an artist for a year, we're entitled to a year of post-term commissions. If we worked with an artist for five years, then we receive five years of diminishing post-term commissions, and so on.

Agents

Next up is the category of agents who handle your live bookings and receive 10 percent of the gross earnings on your live shows income for doing so. Like with anything, some agents go above and beyond, but ultimately an agent's job is to book and negotiate shows. Because this is their primary role, agents are often able to take on far more artists than managers, since management covers all aspects of an artist's career. You and/or your manager want to be a priority for your agent. You can become a priority by getting your agent your estimated release time period and plan as far in advance as possible. This is so they can start getting holds for shows together, as well as pitching you for tours. We've discussed how to really land support slots, so know that doing so is truly a team effort. This can include your manager scoping out if they know anyone on the team of the artists your agent is pitching to support. But know that the real key to landing support slots is you having relationships with other artists, as discussed.

Some US agencies are starting to branch out and handle other territories, but traditionally there are a slew of agencies that operate out of the UK that will handle the "rest of the world" for you. That said, you and your manager want to arm these agents with metrics in addition to your release timeline and plan. You also want your manager to send regular career highlights such as press, synchs, radio play, and any additional promotional elements that are landed to help your agent(s) do their job most effectively.

Both US and international agents pitch artists for festivals. When I was a teenager, I always wondered why the UK and Europe had Glastonbury and Reading/Leeds and the US did not have major festivals. With the debut of Bonnaroo and Coachella at the turn of the century, this has all changed, and the US market is now completely oversaturated with festivals. Despite this, know that these slots are still super competitive. Just like with your regular show strategy, you should start regionally and locally, as playing a street festival in your hometown is a great start and an awesome way to gain new fans who might not know your music otherwise. At the same time, be realistic with your agent. When I start working with an agent, I let them know up front that I'm not going to yell and scream at them demanding the main stage at Lollapalooza. If I do feel the artist has festival potential, I ask the agent if we can put our heads together to find some promoters we know personally who are fans of the artist and collectively decide who we can go after as a team. Don't be someone who freaks out when you land a festival and your name isn't high up enough on the poster or the font of your name isn't large enough. Show some gratitude, and if you keep working hard with a great attitude and create great art and killer live performances, you'll get there.

As your career grows, you may also have a film/TV/web show agent if you score, act, or appear on screen, a literary agent if you want to write or co-write a book, as well as a speaking agent. Major agencies (i.e. William Morris Endeavor or WME, Creative Artists Agency or CAA, Agency for the Performing Arts or APA, and United Talent Agency or UTA) handle all of these aspects. But if there is an independent agent elsewhere who you feel is a better fit for one of these specific categories, you can always ask to carve it out. We have done this successfully in the realm of speaking for our comedy and music clients, where they are repped by a music or major agency for their touring, but a boutique speaking agency to maximize and specialize in that revenue stream. So it's worth a shot if that's of interest.

Business Managers

Business managers are essentially bookkeepers and accountants who specialize in the music and entertainment industries. This can be helpful, as they have an understanding of where your revenue is coming from. They may also be up to help draft tour, live appearance, and recording budgets, plus advise on insurance related to music and entertainment. They also help pay musicians, touring crews, and team members as your career grows. And if they are a certified public accountant, or CPA, they will handle your tax return(s) at the end of the year. The plural is if you have an entity for your art as well as your individual tax return, which we'll discuss later in this section.

At the same time, it is to your benefit to have your own revenue spreadsheet and, even better, to work on it with your business manager. As mentioned, I have plenty of artists who have business managers but who I am constantly finding or creating revenue for. So don't feel like once you have a team in place that you can just put the blinders on and assume that you're receiving all revenue that is owed to you. And I'm not at all saying that reputable business managers are doing this intentionally. However, they are human, and often have many clients. Do yourself a favor and work on the revenue stream spreadsheet in this book with your business manager and check in with them a few times a year to ensure it's updated.

Your business manager can also set you up as a business entity, which is something you should do when you have the funds to do so. This protects you personally from liability professionally. So much so that larger artists often set up additional entities for their touring and recording to keep those revenue streams separate from each other and their personal funds. This is so if god-forbid, you do ever have a legal dispute, a variety of your income streams are protected. As mentioned, a business manager should handle both your personal taxes and your company tax returns if they are a CPA. Make sure that they do and specifically ask to ensure it gets done.

I feel that an artist needs a business manager when they start to ask when they need a business manager. This often means they have questions about their taxes and are paying out a variety of touring and recording royalties and payments to team members. Similar to attorneys, business managers often work for an hourly rate, which ranges, or on a 5 percent gross commission of all earnings.

Label/Distribution Company

We have covered this, but if you have the opportunity and decide to work with a label or distributor, I'll break down these categories briefly again to ensure all potential team members for an artist are covered in this chapter:

- Distribution company: A distribution company, such as The Orchard, Symphonic, or Redeye receives anywhere from a 15 to 25 percent commission on digital revenue for distributing music, depending on the services they are handling. Many of their services (social media strategy, YouTube tagging) are covered in this book, but it can be worth it to pay a higher distribution rate for pitching playlists and writing your release plan, if that is truly overwhelming to you otherwise. That is up to you. Some of these companies have physical distribution arms and will let you know if there is enough demand for your CDs and vinyl to handle that as well.

- Independent label: "Indie" labels are generally 50/50 deals on recording revenue after all expenses have been recouped. Some own your master recordings in perpetuity; others will license your release from you for a set amount of time.

- Major label: A major label will retain roughly 85 percent of your master recordings' revenue and more often than not, own them in perpetuity. It is rare that they don't want a cut of your merchandise, live shows, publishing, and branding revenue as well. However, I do know of artists and managers who have built up an artist's career following the tenets of this book and then had the leverage to license their recordings to major labels for a set period of time. This is an awesome position to be in, though the artists I have in mind often put in years of work on their own to get there.

Publicists, Radio, and Promo Teams

Some labels have in-house PR and radio, but many hire out. You can also hire these independent PR and radio promotions, as discussed. Social media is generally handled by the artist and their management team, though you and your label (if you have one) can also experiment by working with online marketing companies such as Sneak Attack, Fame House and Cyber PR.

Publishing and Synch Teams

You no longer need a publisher in the modern era, as your publishing revenue can now be collected for you by companies such as Songtrust. But plenty of songwriters do have music publishers, and there are great companies out there. Here is a recap of the majority of publishing deal scenarios that are available, generally speaking:

- Administrative or "admin" deal: A publisher receives anywhere from 15 to 20 percent of your publishing revenue to administer and collect on your songwriting for you. Note that these percentages are absolutely negotiable, based on leverage with regard to where you're at in your career. You own and control your rights, which will revert back to you at the end of the term or when your deal recoups and you give them notice per what you agreed to in your contract. Note these dates in your revenue spreadsheet and however you keep track of dates otherwise (say, in a Google Calendar). If you've recouped your deal, it's in your best interest to renegotiate when your term expires and you give notice.

- <u>Co-publishing or "co-pub" deal</u>: A publisher receives upward of 50 percent of your publishing revenue as well as portion of copyright ownership, sometimes for a set amount of time, other times for life. Do not sign a deal like this without an advance cash payment.

- Similarly, many artists have a synch team on board for pitching their music to film, TV/web, and advertising spots. Companies such as Terrorbird, Music Alternatives and Bank Robber receive a 20 to 25 percent commission for doing so on synchs they land and negotiate on your behalf.

Merch Company

It's in your best interest to self-fulfill your online merchandise sales as long as possible. But as you grow, you're most likely going to want to work with a reputable merchandise company, as discussed. This relationship is on you, for the most part. But like we've discussed throughout this book, you should build a relationship with your point person at the merch company. This is so they are working with you to maximize ideas and income.

Team Re-con

I've described how to achieve many of these goals on your own through-out this book. So build up your career to get your team in place. At the end of the day, you ideally want to work with professionals who you feel you have a strong connection with. Additionally, I often hear artists that are in the great position of having multiple team members interested say, "Should I go with this agency or that agency?" or, "This publicist or that publicist?" Trust me, they all know the same people, as well as each other. It's a small industry, and specific genre niches within the industry can be smaller. So find team members who believe in you and your music (though they all do when you have traction, so definitely ask their clients what it's like working with them and also trust your intuition) and that you have a great connection with. As well as someone who you feel you can have a solid regular workflow and working relationship with.

AFTERWORD

W e did it! Now you have, as of this writing, all of my thoughts on how an artist can build a sustainable and long-term music career, not missing a single revenue stream along the way. Until now, I had only presented this information in such a manner once. Why? I'm generally asked to speak on specific areas within this book. But shout out to the Between the Waves music conference in Madison, Wisconsin, who gave me free reign to present on my topic of choice, which became the tenets of this book. Other than that, *no one has ever had access to this information, in this manner, other than the artists I've worked with or team members at our company.* I'm thrilled to have shared what I feel are the best practices for modern tools available to artists in an upfront and clear manner, from creation to execution.

That said, I've also hesitated on writing this book for a long time, knowing that new tools will arise that artists can benefit from. To solve this, we have dedicated https://www.9giantstepsbooks.com/SustainableAfterword[32] to just that. Any time I or someone on one of our teams has a suggestion on a new tool you should be using, we will post it at the aforementioned link.

I truly hope that the information I've laid out is clear and helpful to you. Truth be told, there are whole books and classes at universities on *each*

---

32 https://www.9giantstepsbooks.com/SustainableAfterword

chapter topic that this book covers. So know that if you're looking for a deeper dive, that information is absolutely out there. But I actually don't think you need to know the history of statutory rates or memorize what a mechanical royalty is. You need to know how to build a long-term career and collect on all revenue that is available and owed to you. That said, I'll list some of my favorite resources I can personally vouch for below for those who want a deeper dive:

- Pre-recording Marketing Foundation, Email List, Text Message Club and Social Media, as well as, How to Market With or Without a Budget: Any and everything by Ariel Hyatt of Cyber PR.

- Your Live Strategy and Efficient Touring: Martin Atkins's *Tour Smart* and Ray Waddell's *This Business of Concert Promotion and Touring: A Practical Guide to Creating, Selling, Organizing, and Staging Concerts.*

- When Do I Need an Attorney, Business Manager, and/or a Manager?: Defining an Artist's Traditional "Team": *All You Need to Know About the Music Business* by Donald S. Passman Keep this one handy if you're on a label to understand your deal, including words that amazingly still exist, such as "breakage." Fun fact: I've had the absolute honor of contributing to the last few editions of this book on modern marketing.

Know that there are *countless* more resources on a variety of topics covered in this book, not limited to legal, recording, and music publishing in particular. So on the one hand, if you're interested in educating yourself further, go for it! But if not, I truly believe that we have covered everything you need to know to build a sustainable music career and not miss a single revenue stream along the way. Judging from the overwhelmingly positive reaction upon launching the pre-order for this book, there is clearly demand and thirst for knowledge in this manner.

So tell me how it goes! Keep me posted on what's working for you. Communicating via Twitter[33] is best as I can share your news from there as well. And who knows? If you find this book as useful as we hope that it is, and we fill up a web page of new tools, we're happy to release updated versions as things progress. That said, we're kind of at peak streaming at the moment when it comes to the current format of music. (Unless I, or someone, launches what I feel is a truly equitable and sustainable streaming service for all[34], but one step at a time...)

I got into music because I loved it so much that, as a teenager, when we had to say what we were thankful for on Thanksgiving, I'd say, "Music. And my family," with my uncle joking, "In that order." Artists are why the music industry exists. I have and will continue to devote my career to ensuring that you get everything you deserve and more. So start with this book, let me know how it goes, and I cannot wait to see your career grow and thrive with your incredible art.

33 https://twitter.com/emwizzle
34 https://www.billboard.com/articles/business/6480579/
equal-transparent-streaming-plan-emily-white-guest-post

ABOUT THE AUTHOR

Emily White is an entrepreneur and Founder at Collective Entertainment and #iVoted. White's career spans the entertainment industry, always putting artists and talent first, while taking care of fans a very close second. Her name graced the cover of *Billboard* magazine while in her 20's, with White's work additionally covered by *Forbes*, *Fast Company*, *Bloomberg*, *Rolling Stone*, CNN, Fox Business, *Vox*, *The Huffington Post*, *Pitchfork*, *Relix*, *The Fader*, *Pollstar*, *Stereogum*, *Alternative Press*, ESPN and more. She is a regular speaker around the globe at events such as SXSW, Midem, BIGSOUND Australia, Canadian Music Week, PollstarLive!, NAMM, Music Biz, NARM, SanFran MusicTech, Between The Waves, and innumerous universities. White has served on the boards of Future of Music, Well-Dunn, CASH Music, SXSW, The David Lynch Foundation Live!, The Grammys' Education Committee, and Pandora's Artist Advisory Council. Her first book, *Interning 101*, was released in 2017 (9GiantStepsBooks) and is a coursebook at schools around the world. White is an Adjunct Professor at New York University's Clive Davis Institute of Recorded Music in Tisch School of The Arts.

 @EmWizzle

ACKNOWLEDGEMENTS

Thank you so much to Bob, Ann, and Jesse White; Grandma and Grampa White; Edward and Tish Kehoe; Joyce Dollinger; Cecelia, Ted, Greg, and Maureen Dempsey; Helen Kehoe; Mel, Tiffany, and Bailey Stewart; George Howard, Pompy, and 9GiantStepsBooks; Melissa Garcia, Katrina Bleckley, and all at Collective Entertainment; Sean Lawton; Zachary Rusher; Julia Nunes; Bruce Houghton; Bobby Lord; Kevin Lyman, Don Passman, and Amaechi Uzoigwe; Between the Waves; Jeff Riccio and Wes Bockley at JSR Merchandising; Andy Partridge and Chloe Eglington; Future of Music Coalition; Fox Stevenson, Dan Sawyer, and Bustre; Kelly Nichols; John De Lord at Everpress; Mike Luba, Bob Ezrin, Bill Hein, and John Raso; Amanda Palmer and Brian Viglione; Anna Vogelzang; Mary Lee Eletz; The Wild Honey Pie; Lauren Ross; Craig Snyder; Ajay Gosain; John Schmidt; Karin Koopmans; Jåson Mastrine; Jenni Call; Anne Elizabeth; Ian Hicks; Tommy Marz; Tymothee Harrell; Lydia Bowman; Jes Allen, Hannah Ehrlich, Irmghard Gehrenbeck, Stuart Heys, Christie Adema, Yelena Reydman, William Defebaugh, and all from The Tailwind Jungle Retreat.

Made in USA - Kendallville, IN
1128804_9780999331620
06.29.2020 0932